HUMOR POWER

How to Get It, Give It, and Gain

HUMOR POWER

How to Get It, Give It, and Gain

by HERB TRUE
with ANNA MANG

DOUBLEDAY & COMPANY, INC.
Garden City, New York
1980

ISBN: 0-385-14618-3
Library of Congress Catalog Card Number 79–55370
Copyright © 1980 by Herb True and Anna Mang

In Memory of Betty Dick

The TEAM and I miss her and
remember her humor power. We
dedicate this book to her.

Foreword

More than a moment's pleasure, even more than a method of relaxation, the power of humor can become a positive force in your life. You can use it, with enthusiasm. You can use it to solve problems. You can use it to win.

In this book, Dr. Herb True imparts some secrets toward enhancing your humor power and strengthening its use. Joy, he notes, is part of the power of humor.

It's no secret that I personally believe in the power of joy and enthusiasm to inspire achievement. In my writing and in my speaking, whether as a lecturer or as minister of Marble Collegiate Church, I regularly emphasize that power.

I believe, too, that when you express joy and enthusiasm, through your humor power, you can play a vital role in the decade ahead.

During what has been called the "Me Decade" of the seventies, much was said and written about narrow, limited aims. I always felt that perhaps those who shouted "Me, me, me!" focused inwardly, toward themselves. They ignored goals to pursue wants. They forgot about the full potential which they possess.

Not everyone accepted the "Me" idea. By no means. Throughout the seventies, I observed a considerable resurgence of quite a different philosophy—happy, idealistic, full of spiritual joy in living. The eighties will, in my opinion, see an even greater blossoming of this philosophy.

The "Us Decade," perhaps? More accurately, and not just in the grammatical sense, we might call the eighties the "You Decade." That means you as an individual, you with others, you as a child of God. It means you, giving of yourself to others. It is you, for others.

Does being for others mean putting aside your personal objectives? Indeed, no. Individuals who espouse the "Me" attitude are saying, "I'm for me—and against you, because you may interfere with my narrow, cynical wants." Believe me, if you think that way, you're against yourself, against your own fulfillment, against your richer opportunities to lead, to achieve, to win.

The "You" philosophy says you can—indeed, you should —become personally successful in the little things and in the larger ones. Your power to give inspiration to others returns to enrich you. That is part of the Lord's purpose—His goal for you.

Where does the power of humor enter into all this? A point of view turned inward, toward the self, breeds pomposity and squelches humor. When joy flows outward from the self, to others, humor's power works for you.

Jesus Christ Himself is against gloominess and for joy. Certainly, He is against pomposity. When He told us about those who take care to pray prominently in church or publicly on a street corner, He spoke ironically. Reverently we may say that He put His humor power to work, to deflate hypocrisy and pomposity.

In gathering illustrations for the positive results of living enthusiastically, I've seen some exciting examples of people who overcame difficulties and surmounted barriers—because they were excited by the power of joy. They didn't have time to be grim or pompous. They were too busy trying, and achieving.

Once again, I believe that you have the power to realize your full potential in the world of the eighties. Indeed, you can help to shape and revitalize that world. The joyful power of humor will help you.

Just how do you go about expanding and using your humor power? That is what Herb True tells you in this book.

It will amuse you, in your lighthearted moments, and give you more such moments. It reminds you not to take yourself too solemnly.

The book is full of sound ideas for those who take their job in life seriously. With guidelines and examples, it reveals some of the ways you can use humor power to influence and inspire others, to make yourself memorable, and to win greatness.

It's a practical book. In all aspects of everyday life, its simple suggestions will help you to get the best results, whether standing in line at the supermarket, speaking to a group of salespeople, or tackling the difficult job of getting others to accept change.

I believe that it can help you create and use humor power to your lasting advantage. Herb True is an inspiring friend of mine, and he comes through with his engaging personality in this book.

NORMAN VINCENT PEALE

Acknowledgments

In all of your relationships, you can be as effective and as successful as your associates and your humor power enable you to be. This truth, I believe, is most important.

Although every individual develops and applies the unique power of humor in his own way, it is always amplified by teamwork. I wanted to write this book to share with you some ideas and approaches developed with TEAM. Together, this team of associates and I create, adapt, and polish humor material. Then, we apply humor as humor power, through presentations for a wide variety of audiences—in business, industry, education, religion, or government, for instance.

Our humor materials are specially focused for the specific needs of each audience. And this you-directed, or audience-directed, focus makes the difference between humor and humor power.

Now, a little background.

TEAM International of South Bend, Indiana, creates visual/verbal presentations about such central themes as creativity, communication, leadership, and motivation. My role is to deliver those presentations throughout this country and abroad. TEAM coined the term "Edu-Tainer" to define my role as a speaker and psychologist who reinforces education with entertainment.

Some of the members of our TEAM are:

Don Norton, research and humor adviser, and Connie Hume, ideas and humor researcher. Betty Dick, whose recent death has saddened both TEAM and me greatly, was my humor writer and consultant for eighteen years. She was the most ingenious, most creative humor-material writer, researcher, and consultant I have ever known. If a humor-powered message in these pages especially appeals to you, it's probably because Betty, Don, or Connie came up with a quip or story that made the message come alive.

Thelma Howard, program manager who schedules and arranges for all presentations, co-ordinated the activities involved in writing the book.

Donna Simmons, research associate, who follows up on the details and results of presentations, followed through on the organization of humor materials and humor-power applications.

Jim Pickens, visuals co-ordinator, helps us see the power in humor. Aside from his TEAM activities, Jim is a speaker who, in a section of this book, has shared some ideas with you.

You have your own teams, of private-life family and friends and public-life associates on the job. Your interest in reading these words suggests that you enjoy humor and use it to advantage. It's my belief that greater rewards will spring forth when you transform your humor into dynamic humor power, and this book offers some specific ways you can do it.

Because life is easier if we can experience an in-fun mood from time to time, I hope, too, that you will enjoy some smiles and chuckles as you read.

Thanks for sharing our TEAM's interests!

Herb True

Contents

HUMOR
POWER

How to Get It, Give It, and Gain

1 The Power
of Humor

The baby's crying, breakfast is burning, the kids won't listen to teacher, the congregation doesn't listen to preacher, the sales force didn't make the quota, the consumers are complaining about what they bought, the boss is cross and so is the staff, your co-workers won't carry their share of the load, and things in general are falling apart.

Even worse, it may seem, that big promotion, honor, or reward you counted on has fallen through.

To cope with these and other challenges of everyday life, you need power—whether you're parent or child, teacher or taught, minister or ministered to, seller or customer, boss or employee, manager or the managed. The question is, what kind of power?

As an idea, power permeates our lives. Perhaps a dozen or more times a day, we hear, read, or speak of it. We talk about American Power, Community Power, Power Resources, Black Power, Power Shortages, Power Blocs, the Powers that Be, and More Power to Me! We may even mention Willpower, the Power of the Human Mind, and Spiritual Power.

As a force, power fascinates us and always has. The search for it has beckoned humanity to goals of good—and goals of greed. Dictators, past and present, have grabbed power and wielded it to control others, to dominate and destroy. And that kind of power does destroy—those who use it!

If what you want is merely the power to control what people do, either a carrot or a stick will work. The carrot of praise or a raise or the stick of punishment will persuade many people to *act* the way we believe they should.

Whether they will *think* the way we hope they will sparks a different problem. Individuals do need appreciation and recognition, and words of praise or cash rewards can help to answer these needs. But cash seems cold and praise empty unless we can affirm such rewards with warm feeling and you-directed thought. Praise then becomes heartfelt, and cash changes into a symbol for achievement which goes beyond the mere mechanics of performance.

From the you-directed viewpoint, we might find that power is as positive, or as negative, as we are. We can be power mad, or we can do a powerful lot of good! It depends on whether we have power, or power has us.

Power holds you and me in a negative grip when we think, "If only I could get my family, my friends, my on-the-job associates, or the people next door to do what *I* want." This kind of thinking may cause others to go through the motions of seeming to do what we want, without actually giving us what we need.

The best way we can get what we need from others is to give them what *they* need! Over and over, this message has come from widely differing fields of psychological thought. Some psychologists may refer to the conditioning of moods or the reinforcement of behavior. And some may talk in terms of the need to see through another's eyes or to get involved with another's problems and hopes. Whatever the approach, the direction leads toward the same goal: improving our understanding of others, and ourselves. I believe the power of humor can help us reach this goal. But before I can begin to offer some guidelines, you and I need to exchange a few questions and answers.

What is humor power? Is it the same thing as a sense of humor? And what is humor? For now, let me answer with some dictionary-style definitions.

Humor is a quality which can evoke mirth, cause merriment, or entertain in a pleasurable way.

A sense of humor is the ability to recognize and express humor.

And *humor power* is the art of using your sense of humor, and applying humor, to improve your relationships with others *and* your straightforward evaluation of yourself.

Now, one more question and answer. How did I learn about humor power? In my professional life as a speaker, teacher, and research psychologist, I have learned by giving humor power. When I was a professor at the University of Notre Dame, I gained humor power from my students, and I continue to gain it today from my audiences and the TEAM of associates who help me create my lecture-platform presentations. In fact, our TEAM coined the term "Edu-Tainer"—educator/entertainer—for me to express our belief that humor power reinforces learning. (And the name of our organization, True Education And Motivation, expresses our goals in an easy-to-remember way, while affirming our dedication to teamwork.)

In my personal life, I share humor power with Betty Ann, my wife and partner, and our eight children. And I've learned far more about humor power from our kids than I've ever taught them.

Based on my own experience, it's my belief that we can discover how to:

Press the Button!

Just as turning on a switch sends electricity along a wire, pressing our humor-power button can move a unique energy along a channel. We channel humor power toward direct communication with others.

Humor—and Humor Power

With humor, we can learn to laugh at trouble. Through humor power, we can lift ourselves and others above trouble.

In fact, the boiler room for humor power is located in our emotions, not our intellect. Your humor power is you, revealed in a favorable light. It expresses the warmth of your being, the generosity of your nature, the charity of your heart.

True humor springs not more from the head than from the heart; it is not contempt. Its essence is love.

—THOMAS CARLYLE

In all the situations of daily life, humor is the power you must have if you want to make a meaningful difference in your view of your own goals and in your relationships with others. Use humor's power to help others and you'll find you're helping yourself to a more rewarding life. This power bridges the gulf between "them" and "you" by bringing "them" closer to "you."

Humor power is a must for motivators and communicators, vital for managers and leaders, a plus for teachers, preachers, salespeople, and parents, and a bonus for everyone who wishes to lighten the load of life's burdens. It's a bonus we can give to everyone we meet.

Humor can ease strain, oil relationships, underline points, reduce tensions, relieve pressures, and generally enhance the quality of life. It draws us out of our shells, relaxes us in the company of other people, breaks the ice, and gains us friends. It energizes us with confidence and saves us from embarrassment in many an unpleasant moment.

HUMAN ENCOUNTERS
—HUMOR-POWERED!

Most human encounters offer the opportunity to use humor power. That's the case whether the encounter happens between individuals or between one individual and his emotions. First, let's examine some person-to-person encounters.

When we can treat ordinary problems with lightness instead of antagonism, our humor power inspires trust.

For example, there's the service-station attendant who said, "Shall I fill it up or run it over?"

In a simple, effective, and humor-powered way, he communicated this message: "Trust me, I won't 'run it over'—or goof in any other way that could annoy you."

When we want to complain, we'll most likely be heard better if we use humor power. Consider the customer who told a waiter, "I have a way you can sell thirty per cent more orange juice. Just fill up the glass."

With humor power, the customer implied disappointment —without causing discomfort to the waiter. He may not get more orange juice, but he will get friendly, cheerful service and a warm welcome next time he eats at the same restaurant.

A humor-powered comment, instead of a complaint, will improve your chances of getting better service in almost any situation, from ordering food to protesting about a defective product.

Humor power can help us avoid arguments with others. Here's one example:

"Are you in favor of the new zoning law?" a householder asked his neighbor.

"Well, some of my friends are for it, and some are against it," the neighbor said. "I'm for my friends!"

In a friendly way, the neighbor implied, "Let's agree to disagree." If an issue is controversial or a subject is touchy, we can follow the neighbor's lead. And our humor power will give us another way of saying, "I'm not ready to commit myself," or "Now is not the time to discuss that subject."

Humor power can help us turn negatives into positives by relaxing person-to-person tensions. For example:

A hotel clerk said, "Sorry, all of our rooms are occupied."

And a traveler asked, "If the President were coming, would you have a room for him?"

"Of course," said the clerk.

"Well, he isn't coming," the traveler replied. "So can't you let me have his room?"

The probable result is that the traveler will get a room or the clerk will call other hotels to find one for him. When we need to change another's attitude from no to yes, humor power works to persuade.

And now, let's focus on another kind of human encounter. How can humor power help an individual handle discouragement or other painful emotions? Here are two illustrations:

Humor power turns losers into winners by putting problems or losses in proportion. Take the football coach who had just suffered defeat in a major game. Asked when he felt the turning point occurred, the coach replied, "Right after the national anthem." Like the coach, we can apply humor power to ease the impact of painful reality, cope with discouragement, and see a loss or problem as a temporary short circuit, not a total power failure.

When we can kid ourselves about something that seems very serious to us, we will approach the peak of humor power.

Learn from a college student surveying the wreck of a new motorcycle: "Well, I always said I'd have a motorcycle one day. Now I've had a motorcycle, one day."

To the student, the wreck was a serious matter, yet he refused to take it too seriously. If, in a moment of pain, embarrassment, or disappointment, *you* refuse to take the thing that happened to you too seriously, you will, in that instant, capture the power of humor.

Humor power liberates. It gives us the freedom to be ourselves, to reflect our beliefs and reveal our feelings. With its invigorating energy, we can show that we are free to take risks, willing to be different, and able to make a difference.

Some people laugh at the idea of humor power. They condemn it as frivolous or, at most, speak well of it only as an off-hours relaxation having no place in the serious business of life. They believe that humor power is beneath them when, in truth, it's so far above them that they can't reach to grasp it. Such people could be compared to concrete—all mixed up and fixed in place.

Dorothy Parker, humorous writer, once listened patiently while a nonhumorist expounded views.

Said the humor-powerless one, "I can't bear fools."

Said she, "Oh? That's funny. Your mother could."

Most people, though, value humor power. It's what you and I admire in our friends and criticize in our enemies—because they don't have it. It's what we use when we sting those enemies with a half-caress.

We want to work with and for a person who reflects it and spend our lifetime in marriage with a person who has it. Business and industry consider humor power essential in managers. Students crave it from teachers. We appreciate it in our leaders. Politicians capitalize on it at election time. Children thrive on it when their parents and playmates constantly expose them to it. But some unfortunate children have never seen their parents smile or heard them laugh.

PERSONALLY YOURS—HUMOR POWER

Humor's power is special, individual, and personal to you and your role in life. How can you put it to work to expand your personality and enjoy more successful business, family, and social relationships?

The upcoming chapters offer specific examples. For now, let me invent some things that might happen during a typical day to a mythical "you" and let me show how humor power can help.

8 HUMOR POWER

Alert: I've included two situations where humor is short-circuited. Look for them!

You oversleep—and wake up to smell breakfast burning. You have a choice. Grumble, gripe, and growl. Or, pull your humor power together and ask your mate, "Okay, what are you going to throw in my cage for breakfast this morning?"

A bitterly angry neighbor storms at you as you leave for work on a bitter-cold morning. Your neighbor can't move his car because your car is parked too close to it. Or so your neighbor says.

Again, you have a choice. Say to your neighbor, "There's plenty of room, dingaling. Why don't you get your eyes examined?" Or, smile and apologize: "Sorry. It was so cold this morning, I couldn't get my wife/husband moving." (And move your car!)

On your job, you find your boss or associates dithering about a mountain of molehills. Your humor power can soothe and smooth. Put worries and problems in proportion by saying, "Remember, if we went through last year's file marked 'Important,' probably the only thing we'd keep would be the paper clips."

At lunch, your associates are still tense, even quarrelsome. You want to relax their tensions, prevent arguments, and help them forget about business worries. Tell a joke on yourself.

"Yesterday at lunch, I asked the man at the next table, 'Do you want to buy some widgets?' 'No,' he answered, 'why on earth should I?' 'Well, I wanted to say I talked business at lunch,' I told him, 'so the meal would be tax-deductible.'"

A nervous associate is climbing the walls about a speech he will make at an afternoon meeting. Put him at ease with a few humorous remarks.

"Don't worry. Just laugh—if anyone tells you, 'As a speaker, you're not a total loss. You can always serve as a bad example!'"

Or: "If you goof, try telling them this. 'I'm always putting my foot in my mouth. Even my toothpaste comes from Dr. Scholls.'"

At home again, you face a family argument. With humor, your college-student son asks, "Did you know that according to anthropologists man was not meant to walk upright?" You reply, "So?" And he says, "So lend me the keys to the car."

But you decide you need the car, and . . .

You go to a party, where some clumsy oaf upsets a drink on you. You can make a scene, berate the upsetting person, or smile and say, "Don't worry. I'm not burning."

Did you spot the two short circuits in that typical day?

The first one happened when "you" tried to put your speech-making associate at ease, with funny remarks. Chances are, he wasn't prepared or conditioned to accept a joke on himself in that moment of anxiety.

You can best relieve his anxiety by kidding yourself. Quip the same quips, but as examples of what you did when *you* spoke at a meeting.

The second short circuit occurred when "you" didn't respond to the humor of your college-student son. "You" might say yes, give him the car keys, and get a lift from a friend, or take a cab to the party. But if "you" must say no, a chuckle or a smile will signal appreciation of the son's humor and keep your communication going.

When we get humor from others and give it in return, with smiles, words, or other signals, we set the humor-power cycle moving toward better communication.

"Handle with Care"

Like most forms of power, humor might be labeled "Handle with Care." Carelessly handled, it can interrupt our communication cycle.

When humor is aggressive, biting, sarcastic, or scornful, we may get others to laugh. But we won't help them think better of us or influence them in any affirmative way. Humor can be happy, robust, and dynamic. Then, it has the power to generate lightness, victory, success, and a wealth of vital energy.

Humor power shows us not only what we are but what we can become. It strips away false pride or vanity and opens our eyes to our illusions, our superficial views, our sometimes-skewed values.

Once we develop humor power, can we handle its self-illuminating energy? We can, when our humor power is grounded in a realistic outlook. We can turn it on our own actions and use it to achieve a balance between seriousness and fun.

This priceless power inspires us to study our faults objectively. It endows us with a detachment that keeps us from getting an inferiority complex, and encourages the growth of proportion and perspective.

FUELED BY FUN AND PLAY

Where can you and I go to get some humor power? That's the subject of this book. (You didn't think I would tell you all my secrets in this first chapter, did you?)

We weren't born with it; we can't buy it. Before we can "press the button," we must create and develop our individual humor power.

We can start by revving up our spirit of fun and play. That's the spirit that helps us focus our humor power on others by turning it on ourselves. Playfully and in fun, we can disclose more of ourselves while circumventing the pain of self-disclosure. Fueled by the spirit of fun and play, our humor power says, "I'm a fun person. You can laugh with me. And since I can laugh at myself, you can be sure I won't laugh at you. You can trust me."

People around you will discover your fun-filled nature, and they will like, trust, and communicate with you. In the climate of mutual trust, others will feel that they have someone who will listen to them. They will know that they can disclose their troubles and frustrations without the risk of being laughed at or the fear of being ignored.

Give It Away—and Gain

It's inevitable. Give your humor power as a bonus to others, and you just can't keep from gaining bonuses of your own.

You'll gain prestige because people trust you and like to be around you. You'll gain the power to get on top of any situation—a sure road to success. You'll gain many of the things money can buy, and many more that can't be purchased anywhere.

Throughout history, much of what mankind achieved came from the transformation of a playful, fun-filled spirit into humor-powered energy. Without it, we couldn't have coped. Certainly, it has helped us extend our reach beyond our grasp.

I believe this power flows from our Creator. Surely God intended us to develop our humor power. As some biblical scholars suggest, a perfectly solemn Being couldn't possibly have imagined mankind!

Great pioneers, statesmen, and other leaders reached out to their greatness with the help of humor. In America, we think immediately of Benjamin Franklin and Abraham Lincoln as leaders who lightened their burdens with humor and shared humor with others.

Scientists, inventors, and other explorers have improved the quality of our lives with their discoveries. But even when they seemed totally serious, we know that they must have possessed humor power. On the way to great discoveries, it's essential to take lightly the setbacks that inevitably precede success.

How much more we could do if only all of us—collectively—and each of us—individually—would explore, cultivate, develop, and exercise our humor power! As we increase the ways we use that power to help others, we will be remembered better and more lastingly—a goal each of us hopes to achieve.

When we connect our humor power to others, it won't help us to control or dominate. It will help us to communicate, and that's the truly serious business of life, be it personal, family, social, business, or professional life. Communication means giving and gaining. It moves from you to me and then returns from me to you. As the law of reciprocity puts it, the more you give, the more you gain. Through humor-powered giving and gaining, we can motivate, influence, and inspire.

Humor power goes deeper than laughter, yields more riches than a smile, delivers more returns than a giggle or a grin. It isn't necessarily laugh-provoking. One way to begin generating it is to explore just what humor is.

2 What Is Humor?

The simplest answer to this question could be another question: "Who knows?" No one does know for sure, although some of our greatest minds—among them Aristotle, Sigmund Freud, Don Rickles—have sought the answer. Humorists and students of humor can't define it precisely, or at least they usually can't agree to accept the same definition. We might say then that humor is controversial.

Written controversy about humor goes back to Plato and his Dialogues, some three or four centuries before Christ. Humor should be avoided, Plato wrote, because it is founded only on the pleasure we get from laughing at the pain of others.

Over the centuries, philosophers, psychologists, scientists, humorists, and other experts agreed and disagreed with Plato. They argued about whether humor is painful, pleasurable, or a combination of both; purely emotional, totally intellectual, or an intellectual/emotional blend; physiological, psychological, or both.

A definition I like says that humor brings pleasant relief from painful experiences and emotions. But that's one definition among many.

Back in 1901, James Sully, English philosopher, said

about humor, "Hardly a word in the language . . . would be harder to define than this familiar one."

Things haven't changed much since the turn of the century. "Different Jokes for Different Folks," an article in *Psychology Today,* January 1979, analyzed the results of a humor survey conducted among the magazine's readers. "Humor is a subtle and elusive phenomenon," authors James Hassett and John Houlihan pointed out, and, "There is no definitive list of 'kinds of humor.'"

Since laughter can be seen and heard, it is examined and tested more often than the elusive quality of humor. In an attempt to pin down what humor is, researchers measure laughter by counting the rates of respiration and the vibrations of the diaphragm.

A typical description of measured laughter is quoted by Patricia Keith-Spiegel, psychologist, educator, and contributor of the opening chapter in *The Psychology of Humor.* The description covers, among other details, spasms of the diaphragm, movements of the upper body, dilations of the nostrils, bulging of the eyes, and vibrations of the jaw. "Upon reading [this] objective description of laughter," Keith-Spiegel observes, "one gets the feeling that a person engaging in this act must be critically ill rather than enjoying himself."

Although we may smile about laughter tests, we can empathize with the researchers and be grateful to them. They're trying! And their results do show that laughter plays a happy role. We catch humor from others, and laughing helps us spread the contagion.

Even if we can't define humor precisely, we can form some opinions about it. And one of them is:

YOU'RE THE EXPERT

Humor is where you find it. It grows as you become expert at sharing it. Then it develops into a unique, totally self-created facet of your personality. You're an expert when you express humor through your "sixth sense"—your sense of humor.

Traditionally, this sense is located in our funny bone, or elbow. That's an appropriate place for it! If we bump our elbow against something, the resulting sensation tells us a lot about the pain that lies at the root of humor.

If one of our five senses is impaired, we lose part of our contact with life. If we neglect to develop our sixth sense, we lose much of our emotional balance and our ability to relate to others. Yet our valuable sense of humor is only one of the ingredients that fuels our humor power. We also need a spirit of fun and play, honesty in projecting our feelings, and empathy with other individuals.

When you can combine and apply these ingredients, you'll turn humor into humor power. And you'll become a real expert.

On the way to humor power, you'll discover that humor is not only controversial, it's paradoxical. For example, we can't put humor in a package or store it in a container for release at certain times under certain conditions. That's because current or timely humor can make points most effectively, but today's timely news is tomorrow's old story.

Yet, paradoxically, we can recapture and recharge current humor. Even old, outdated humor can be renewed and reused through our individual approaches.

WHAT'S SO FUNNY?

Defining humor may seem easy compared to the problem of deciding what "funny" means. As William James, philosopher and psychologist, described it, analyzing what's funny is like dissecting a frog in a laboratory. After you've finished, nothing remains.

Information tests uncover wide differences of opinions about what's funny. In the *Psychology Today* survey, 14,500 of the magazine's readers gave their opinions of thirty jokes. "Every single joke had a substantial number of fans who rated it 'very funny,' while another group dismissed it as 'not at all funny,'" authors Hassett and Houlihan wrote.

Once again, you're the expert—because funny is *when,* instead of *what.* It's when humor lifts and lightens your spirits and just naturally makes you feel glad and good. Funny is when you react happily and affirmatively to others' humor. And funny is when you can help others feel happy, too.

We can discover more about what's funny when we consider the types and forms of humor. Sometimes, we confuse humor with comedy, but the purpose of comedy is to get laughs, while the best of humor aims for much more—amusement, happiness, joy, merriment, and, but not always, laughter.

Countless types of humor are open to us—among them, the ludicrous or the ridiculous, the incongruous or the unexpected, hyperbole, parody, satire, irony, ridicule, and sarcasm. Sometimes one type of humor may seem much like another, but subtle differences show that humor's exact nature is indeed elusive.

Ludicrous humor, for instance, suggests an underlying pathos, exemplified by the circus clown who dresses and behaves in a funny manner and ends up being drenched by water from an elephant's trunk. While we laugh about his antics, we can identify with the clown and pity him for his troubles.

Ridiculous humor, on the other hand, connotes zaniness, as in the riddle "Where do you get dragon milk?" Answer: "From a cow with very short legs." The incongruous comment tends to be out of place, while the unexpected one is out of tempo. Another way to unexpected humor is through the . . .

Surprise Twist

A line from Will Rogers gives us an example of the surprise twist.

"I'm not a member of an organized political party," Will said, then quipped—"I'm a Democrat."

(If it fits, make the switch to "Republican.")

The forms of humor are infinitely varied—one-liner, quip, wisecrack, proverb, aphorism, poem, cartoon, caricature, anecdote, story, tall story, to mention just a few. These forms shape humor that's verbal, visual, intentional, or accidental.

Actions, done with or without words, may *seem* funny, but there are no funny actions, just funny and individual ways of looking at them. A person slipping on a banana peel and falling isn't a funny sight—unless we think so!

Mix Up Mirth

Accidental humor often comes from mixed-up words. The accident can consist of just one misspelled word—for example, the famous "THIMK!"—or two or more misspaced words, as in the equally famous sign that reminds us to "PLAN AHEA D."

Mixed up in print, words stimulate hilarity. An example from the headlines: "Herb True Hit with Rotary Club." And from the classified section: "Dog for sale, eats anything, especially fond of children."

Another form of accidentally mixed-up words is the spoonerism, named for William Archibald Spooner, an English clergyman. We produce a spoonerism when we say "Thinkle peep" instead of "People think." Dr. Spooner had a habit of transposing the first letters or syllables of words. Asked about the distance to a neighboring town, he replied, "It's five miles as the fly crows." A modern spoonerism concerns the history professor who accused a student, "You hissed my mystery lectures."

Similar to the spoonerism is the malapropism. That's a form of humor named for Mrs. Malaprop, a character created by playwright Richard Sheridan. Memorably, Mrs. Malaprop said such things as "Illiterate him from your memory."

More recently, movie mogul Samuel Goldwyn popularized this form of humor with malapropisms which were often created for him. He is reputed to have said, "This makes me so sore, it gets my dandruff up," and, more philosophically, "It rolls off my back like a duck."

His associates sympathized when he reported, "I've been

laid up with intentional flu." In a business matter, he promised, "I'm giving you a definite maybe." And when he decided to leave an organization, he announced, "Gentlemen, include me out!"

One story has it that Goldwyn hesitated to title a movie *The Optimist*. "We're intelligent people," he told his associates, "but would the average person know it's about an eye doctor?"

Other ways to humor through words include intentional plays on words and best known of these is the pun.

If we make a pun, we might be told, "You should be put in a punitentiary," a punny mix of two words. Others in the pun family consist of words with different meanings but identical sounds—"Prisoner escapes cell and flees"—or words with very different spellings but similar sounds. An example of the latter instance tells of a court jester who was about to be hung. The king sent word that the jester would be pardoned on a promise never again to make a pun. Joyfully, the jester exclaimed, "No noose is good news!" And there went the pardon. Here, a pun shapes a story or vignette.

Intentional humor may mix words deliberately, invent nonsense words, or blend real and nonsense words.

For the adventures of Alice, Lewis Carroll invented Jabberwocky, a nonsense language. He wrote, " 'Twas brillig, and the slythy toves did gyre and gimble in the wabe." Carroll's nonsense made sense, because it appealed to the youthful spirit of fun and play.

SEEING THE POINT

What word forms of humor do verbally, cartoons and caricatures do visually. A cartoon may have a gag line, and often does, but its essence is in the drawing.

Picture this in cartoon style. A sign on a wall: "God Is Dead—Nietzsche." Underneath that: "Nietzsche Is Dead—God." That's funny to read. At least, I think so. But what breaks me up may not even make you smile!

Scrawled on a wall, the sign gains visual impact from the lettering. As an instrument of humor with broad appeal, it has an added element going for it.

Compared to cartoons, caricature penetrates a little deeper. For example, it exaggerates a feature of a famous face or creates a character to symbolize a meaning or a message. Like the Republicans' elephant or the Democrats' donkey.

RHYMING REASON WITH HUMOR

Humor can be powerful when it's poetic. Even a simple rhyme can demonstrate the truth in humor while it amuses. That's the case with this familiar verse by a nineteenth-century writer, Sarah Josepha Hale.

> Mary had a little lamb,
> Its fleece was white as snow,
> And everywhere that Mary went,
> The lamb was sure to go.
>
> He followed her to school one day;
> That was against the rule;
> It made the children *laugh and play,*
> To see a lamb at school.

The italics are mine, but the words show that Sarah Hale understood the importance of a spirit of fun and play. Mary's little lamb inspired that spirit because it appeared in an incongruous place. It was a funny, because unexpected, sight. Undoubtedly, the children laughed and played because they sympathized with the little lamb who dared to go against the rule.

TELLING TRUTHS WITH HUMOR

Proverbs, aphorisms, quips, and one-liners are related as word forms of humor. In a pithy way, they tell a truth, carry ideas, make points, and shed light on our behavior. They have brevity in common, but subtle differences exist.

Usually, "one-liner" and "quip" mean the same thing; when there is a distinction, it's that one-liners go forth and quips come back. Users of one-liners take the initiative by offering humor to others in one or more lines. For example, you can illuminate a realistic, yet assured, self-image, like the short man who kidded himself, "I can't wear cowboy boots. They cut me under the armpits."

Quippers take the sting out of embarrassing questions or awkward moments by responding with humor. Trade gloom for lightness on the quip exchange. Like the toll-booth attendant who, when a motorist explained, "I only have a twenty," quipped lightly, "That's okay. We don't give change on Thursdays."

Both aphorisms and proverbs tell truths, briefly. An aphorism often draws a comparison to reach a conclusion. For example, a familiar aphorism says, "The more things change, the more they remain the same." Another example: "The more I learn about teen-age togetherness, the more certain I am that it happens when her hair curlers get caught in his hair curlers."

A proverb sheds light on human behavior in an insightful way. Humorist George Ade advised, "In uplifting, get underneath," and "Draw your salary before spending it." Here's an Ade for today: "Never put off until tomorrow what should have been done early in the seventies."

Expanding on a proverb by giving it a twist develops still another type of one-liner. For example: "An apple a day keeps the doctor away, but if you want to be a hermit, try an onion instead."

TELLING TALES WITH HUMOR

Stories, anecdotes, vignettes, and tall tales build to a punch line. Usually, anecdote and story mean the same thing; both are humorous tales. But an anecdote becomes more than a story when it tells a biographical tale about a famous person and carries a philosophical thought.

The vignette condenses an anecdote or story into the

briefest possible form. On the other hand, tall tales expand and exaggerate. Tellers of tall tales make so many ludicrous and ridiculous claims that we realize they're saying "The joke's on me."

Exaggeration equals hyperbole, and sharpens a point. Parent to child: "I've told you a million times not to exaggerate."

Whenever exaggeration appears in humor, parody is often present. It forges a weapon, mighty but benign, for the humorpowerful. In *Don Quixote,* Miguel de Cervantes parodied tales of knighthood and chivalry. He exaggerated the character of Don Quixote, a gentleman who believed he was a knight, then exaggerated the don's adventures. In a familiar adventure, Don Quixote battled enemies, or thought he did. But the enemies were really windmills.

Through parody, Cervantes corrected injustices and changed absurd attitudes of his era. His humor lives on in the belief that, after all, much can be done by "tilting at windmills." Or, in modern terms, we *can* fight city hall! In your individual way, you can apply your humor power to change the world.

Parody can also be a simple, funny rewording of something already written. "Mary had a little lamb," for instance, has been parodied many times, in many verses. If you had a friend named Mary, and wanted to offer her a slice of a roast, you could create a mild form of parody by saying, "Mary, will you have a little lamb?"

Parody blends into satire, a type of humor that mirrors and reflects mankind's follies. We're satirical when we say, "Satire helps us change the way we respond to life, because we are greatly influenced by what we see in our mirrors."

Irony refines satire through understatement. Or it answers a question with a question, developing humor that may be more painful than pleasant. Perhaps the most revealing examples of irony come from the Bible. Both the Old and New Testaments contain ironical wit that is so familiar to us we sometimes fail to recognize it.

The idea of lighting a candle only to put it under a bushel basket is but one of many ironic images created by Jesus Christ.

"The blind leading the blind," "casting pearls before swine," and "wolves in sheep's clothing" also testify to the ironical impact of His words.

In the anthology *Treasury of Great Humor* editor Louis Untermeyer cited the Old Testament book of Job as an example of dialogues that "mount to cosmic irony." "After Job's comforters have failed," Untermeyer wrote, "God succeeds, not by comforting Job, nor even by answering his accusations and appeals, but by withering humor . . . God rebukes Job with questions that are unanswerable."

Sarcasm is satire and irony turned bitter. A wisecrack is a one-liner that intensifies sarcasm: "Go over to the brewery and have them put a head on you"; "If brains were dynamite, you couldn't blow your nose."

Cervantes had a wise thought about this form of humor: "Jests that slap the face are not good jests."

Here I'd like to say a good word for ridicule, a form of humor that was once considered too close to sarcasm for comfortable use. Fifteen or twenty years ago, ridicule was usually acceptable only when kidding one's self: "My head is clear as a bell. In fact, I can hear it ringing." Today I find that ridicule is used more often in our relationships with others because it is used differently—to imply a compliment or open the way for others to tell us about our mistakes.

Let me cite an instance that occurred during my presentation to the Standardbred Trotter and Pacer Meeting. I said to a man in the audience, "Gee, I wish cheap clothes looked good on me."

His coat was man-made suede and beautiful. What I didn't know was that his wife, sitting there with him, had made the coat.

Afterward, she came up to me and said, "I appreciate your kidding, but I have to tell you everybody in the room knew I made that coat for Harry." That made me happy because I felt I had created an atmosphere where she could tell me how I goofed. An atmosphere of that kind can rescue humor and save it from failure. "If I had known you made the coat," I told her, "I would have said something like, 'And he appreciated it so much that he gave you a ring—with a place in it for a stone and everything.' "

When you or I say, "Gee, I wish cheap clothes looked good on me," it's essential that the clothes clearly aren't cheap. Or that you and the person you compliment wear clothes in the same price range, but the other person *does* look better.

Alert: Avoid harsh humor. A similar one-liner straddles the line between ridicule and a wisecrack: "Say, you look great. Where does the person who gives you his clothes buy them?" If we use this one-liner, we may put ourselves in the unhappy position of laughing at others for what they are—poor—instead of laughing with them for what they do—wear cheap clothes.

These, then, are some of the types and forms of humor—some scratches on the surface of its depths. They exist for us to use, or not use, as we develop our humor power.

HUMOR AND HOW

Although humor power is complex, you can begin to generate it through some simple, basic approaches.

Think funny. Grasp a situation, turn it inside out or upside down, look at it from a new angle, and see the funny side of it—even if it's a seemingly hopeless situation.

Where can you find your "think funny" ideas? Help yourself to those you find in this book. What's more, the whole world of humor is yours!

Feel free to borrow the pithy proverbs, the sparkling sayings, the joyous jokes of others. Then change, adapt, personalize, and make the material your own. An old joke is one that isn't funny. A new one is any joke that hasn't been told yet in your individual way.

Abe Lincoln knew humor is often more powerful when it's borrowed and quoted. Typically, he remarked, "An old man once told me, 'Folks who don't have any vices generally don't have many virtues.'" This borrowed remark bought him a lot of mileage.

Through practice, you can develop your own "think funnies." As a simple example, consider the word "lemon." Play around with it, and come up with a surprise twist: "When life gives you lemons, it's time to make lemonade."

Give familiar sayings a turn for the funny: "He's no gentleman. He prefers blondes—and brunettes—and redheads."

When we think funny, we think differently. Like Mary's lamb, we resist meaningless conventions and stifling conformity. We cut through sham and pretense to reach the reality of our existence. From a psychological standpoint, we can find reality, and fulfill ourselves, by reaching out to others. But first, we need to take off our disguises and reveal ourselves. Our think-funny humor can help us remove barriers and disguises.

Thinking funny counteracts hate powerfully. The person who possesses humor power would rather think funny about nothing in particular than hate anything.

A True Thought

It is impossible to be angry and laugh at the same time.

Laugh at yourself and with others, for what they do, not what they are. Self-directed laughter untangles misunderstandings, erases mistakes, dissolves discouragement, and conquers failure. Learn to see the funny side of your own behavior and you'll gain self-esteem because you'll be able to forgive your faults or mistakes.

What's more, your example shows others that self-directed laughter fosters self-confidence. Because you have the courage to laugh at yourself, you will give others the freedom to laugh at themselves. And when you laugh with them, you won't hurt them or make them unhappy—because you've demonstrated that you're a person who can share laughter *with* others, not a critic who laughs *at* others.

Bounding Over Barriers

If you do a good job for others, you heal yourself at the
same time, because a dose of joy is a spiritual cure. It
transcends all barriers.

—ED SULLIVAN

Take yourself lightly, and your job in life seriously. When
we reverse the emphasis, we're in trouble! Immaturity lies in
seeing one's self as the center of the world. Maturity comes
with seeing one's self in proper relation to the whole.

As you develop the ability to put minor or major losses in
proportion, you gain maturity. That's easier to do, of course,
when the losses are minor. If you burn breakfast, or even dinner, you can laugh about it and prepare another meal. But if
you miss a chance for promotion or any major reward, it's
even more important to see your loss in relation to your ultimate goal. You still have the opportunity to achieve and succeed.

When down in the mouth, remember Jonah. He came
out all right.

—THOMAS EDISON

The job you take most seriously will be your relationships
with others. But humor can cast a halo around whatever job
you do to make a living. It enables you to work with enthusiasm, honest endeavor, and courage. It lifts the most boring job
into an expression of individuality by putting the stamp of your
unique self on your work.

Make others laugh, and make them happy. By doing or
saying amusing things you spread cheer all around. You'll find
that you have the power to do this when you've learned how to
laugh at yourself. Others will recognize and appreciate you as
a person who can take a joke—especially when it's on you.

GRADUATE TO THE THIRD DEGREE!

I believe that humor power offers three degrees. The first and lowest exists among those who laugh and think funny only about their own jokes.

A second and higher degree appears among persons who laugh and think funny only about the jokes of others.

Highest and finest of all is the degree attained by those individuals who laugh at and think funny about themselves. When we can reach the third degree, problems have a comforting habit of diminishing in importance.

The suggestions I've listed are basic to humor and its power. Much more is involved, of course, and as we continue together through these pages, I will share other step-by-step ways to develop and use your humor power.

If I needed to put humor power into a capsule, I would say that it combines a sense of recognition with relevance. Its power hums along the channels of communication, and we recognize it as relevant and respond to it.

Let's summarize:

Herb's How-To for Humor Power

Think funny. Learn to see the funny side of most any situation.

Laugh at yourself, and with others, for what they do, not what they are.

Take yourself lightly, and your job in life seriously. Discover that life's anxieties and burdens are lighter, less severe than they may seem in relation to the whole.

Make others laugh, and make them happy, by doing and saying amusing things.

And let's develop our humor power—by using it!

3　How to Use Your Humor Power

If you would discover the full potential of humor power to help you weather life's storms, relate to others, and attain your goals, put this unique power to work. The key word is "work"! Humor power doesn't just happen. It takes planning and practice to create and develop it.

But be encouraged. Humor is easier to recognize than it is to analyze—a fact that will help you create humor power by using humor. When you put humor to work, you can judge the way others respond to it and, if necessary, vary your way of using it. And the more you use it, the better it thrives. Prove this to yourself. Connect and direct humor power toward personal, family, and on-the-job life, then see what happens.

Develop a New PERSPECTIVE

What do I mean by "perspective"? Well, show me a man who says he always has his feet firmly planted on the ground, and I'll show you a man who puts his pants on over his head! With his feet-on-the-ground attitude, this man hopes to suggest, "You can't fool me. I never make silly mistakes."

Chances are he's a practical but literal-minded person who can't see that being too practical or too literal may cause silly mistakes. Although he won't actually try to put his pants on over his head, he may reverse other priorities and make serious mistakes—until a different perspective helps him think funny about life's problems, take himself lightly, and laugh at himself.

Your perspective is the way you look at life, at the people you know and meet, and, most of all, at yourself. Focus a new perspective on embarrassing, discouraging, or troubled situations, and you can:

Generate Self-Confidence

Suppose your do-it-yourself hairdo flops. Don't hide your head in the sands of embarrassment. Try telling your friends, "I think I grabbed the electric mixer instead of the blow dryer."

Or, when the barber is giving you a haircut, perhaps he gets carried away—and so does too much of your hair. Stay ahead with humor power. Explain, "The barber did tell me how to save my hair. He even gave me a broom and a paper bag."

What if that stack of papers you're holding slips out of balance? Suddenly, you're doing a juggling act—without success. Regain *your* balance with humor power. Confide, "I promised my doctor I'd give up butter. Now I'm margarine-fingered."

Observe a man/woman situation. "You," a man, may disagree with "her"—a female acquaintance, friend, relative, or associate—about women's liberation. You could antagonize her with this: "I know women aren't the weaker sex. It takes six men to carry a man to his grave, and only one woman to put him there." Instead, try embracing her with humor power. Say, "I'm glad we're now having sexual equality in all areas. This morning, my wife was discussing that very point—with her Avon man."

If you're the woman in this situation, liberate his attitudes with your humor power. You could comment, "I realize women's liberation has its humorous side. I heard about a wedding where the parson pronounced a couple 'person and person.'"

Take a common gardening situation: Your garden is the biggest on the block—the biggest failure. Admit to your neighbors, "Not everyone who has a green thumb is a good gardener. I'm better at sloppy painting."

Raising Laughter

An onion can make people cry, but there has never been a vegetable invented to make them laugh.

—WILL ROGERS

From people like Will Rogers—the noted, the famous, the great—you and I can learn a lot about using humor power in daily life. Politicians and statesmen, for instance, have long known how to turn a fresh perspective on embarrassment or discouragement to their advantage.

Franklin in Dutch with French

Humorist and diplomat Benjamin Franklin sat in the French Academy, listening to an enthusiastic speech. The speaker finished. Everyone else applauded and Franklin joined in.

He didn't understand French, so he asked what the speaker had said. The speech, he learned, had consisted entirely of praise—for Franklin.

With humor power, Ben Franklin overcame his embarrassment by later telling the joke on himself.

Half Empty—and Full

Performers, too, employ a humor-powered perspective in discouraging moments.

Humorist and pianist Victor Borge, when appearing in Flint, Michigan, once faced a house that was no more than half filled. Naturally, he was disappointed. But he advanced to the footlights and remarked to the audience, "Flint must be a very wealthy town. I see each of you bought two or three seats."

And the half-empty house was filled with laughter.

Thanks, Enemies!

Through a fresh perspective, leaders help others to accept them in spite of differing opinions and attitudes. Here's an example from the world of big labor.

When I. W. Abel had just been elected president of the United Steel Workers, he spoke to a group in Johnstown, Pennsylvania—a group that, for the most part, had angrily opposed him and voted for his opponent.

Said Abel, "Thank you for your fine support. Without it, I could not have been elected."

Then the antagonistic audience laughed—and was with him.

From all these examples, we discover how to:

Let Off Steam, Slowly

All of us have pet peeves about government and politics. Why grouse, gripe, and grumble? Let the humor power of quips and one-liners become your escape valve.

After all, in Russia, people can complain about the government all they want—once. That's if they first give their names, addresses, and telephone numbers.

A Russian one-liner says, "The Soviet Union bought the Sahara Desert, and in five years, there was a shortage of sand."

Simmer down, and let off steam, slowly, with thoughts such as these:

"In America, we wonder how we can teach our kids the value of money, when we can't even teach our congressmen."

"Ours is a great country—where anyone can have a second home, a second car, a second TV. Just get a second job, a second mortgage, and a second wind."

"During his years in Washington, our congressman has done the work of two men. Laurel and Hardy."

"We're overlooking one of the biggest sources of natural gas in the country—politicians."

"Even the kids don't play post office any more. It's too slow."

You're annoyed about taxes and inflation. That's news? Switch off squawks and turn on smiles. Air your annoyance and polish your points the humor-powered way:

"The average citizen is one who insists on better roads, bigger schools, more Social Security—and lower taxes."

"Would you believe that a little more than two hundred years ago we went to war to avoid taxation?"

"It's scary to visit my IRS office. It shares space with a blood bank!"

"If this is a free country, how come I can't afford it?"

"Two can still live as cheaply as one, if one is a vegetarian and the other a nudist on a diet."

"America is the land of miracles. Man cannot live on his income, yet he does."

"If electricity rates rise much higher, a porch light will be a status symbol." But a Chinese proverb also says, "It is foolish to go to bed to save on light, if the result is twins."

You can, in fact, take almost any gripe, any point of disagreement, any wrong or injustice, and use humor power to change things for the better. Perceive problems, and create change, by thinking funny about them from your personal viewpoint.

Do you tend to worry and flurry about some facets of modern life? Humor power can help. Share your perspective, calmly and lightly. Be unflappable! Here's how.

"Blaming TV for violence is like blaming beds for sex."

"A guarantee these days is what tells you a product will last until you need a new one."

"School sports are a vital, educational institution. If it wasn't for the field house, where would they hold graduation?"

"Today, we're worrying about shortages of things our grandparents never heard of."

Open Up the OPPORTUNITY
TO COMMUNICATE

Open up with self-directed laughter, and you'll let others see you as you are. That's important! When we openly and honestly show ourselves to others, we influence them to let us know about their motives, dreams, and goals. And our shared self-knowledge diminishes the distance between us.

It's virtually impossible to be too open with others. The more open we are, the more we can understand others' hidden potential, and the more we can develop the potential in ourselves. However, we can't really open up by complaining and criticizing.

Instead, let humor power help you treat yourself lightly and think funny about yourself. Thus you'll show others you're free to risk a little, reveal mistakes, and be yourself. And you'll open the lines of human communication.

Take Risks!

To be a leader means a willingness to risk—and a willingness to love. Has the leader given you something from the heart?

—HUBERT H. HUMPHREY

Any attempt to use humor carries a risk. It's comparable to plugging a cord into a socket and flipping a switch. We expect the electrical power to work and, usually, it does. But we may be disappointed for reasons ranging from a defective cord to a power failure at the electric plant.

Similarly, you can't count on giving and gaining every time you tell a funny story or make an amusing remark. But you certainly can't gain unless you try. And your chances will improve when you offer humor power from your emotions, instead of sending humor from your intellect.

What's more, you'll discover that "he who laughs first, laughs best," as you communicate more fully with the people in your life.

Golden Rule for Laughter

Whatsoever you would laugh at in others, laugh at in yourself.

—HARRY EMERSON FOSDICK

You're the Target

When you tell your stories and anecdotes, build your vignettes, and set off your quips and one-liners, your safest target is you, yourself. If you laugh at yourself, who's going to resent it, your mother?

As another bonus, an unwritten law says that those who laugh at themselves have a right to kid others. Sir Winston Churchill, who used humor power to lighten the burdens of war, once targeted a political colleague with this remark: "He is a modest man, and he has much to be modest about."

Those in the political arena must expect the shaft, but for most of us in everyday life, Churchill's one-liner becomes more forceful when "he" is changed to "I." Whenever you want to express a criticism, make a complaint, or suggest an improvement, the "I" point of view is ideal.

Set yourself up as the target of your humor power, and you can convey messages and make points without offending. For example:

"An egotist is a person of low taste, more interested in himself than me."

"I'd open my mouth to apologize, only I'm afraid a foot would fall out."

"The happiest moment of my life was when I became president of my own company. I always wanted to fool around with the boss's wife."

"I'm not old. I'm in the prime of life. But it takes me longer and longer to get primed."

"I believe in being positive, I think."

"I'm the kind of friend you can count on. Always around when I need you."

Then, to communicate:

Keep the Lines Clear

Frequently, communication fizzles when its lines get snarled. I can't understand you, and you certainly can't understand me, because neither of us is expressing ourselves clearly. Humor's high voltage sparks a special danger here. When we quip, joke, and kid, it's our responsibility to make our meaning exact. Otherwise, painful confusion can result.

Confusion occurs because communication involves far more than the exchange of words. Feelings and moods may transmit unspoken signals that tell others, "You aren't getting through to me." But words can help us move beyond the threshold of negative signals.

Psychologically, we need to consider what our words say about our feelings—and how words bear upon the feelings of other individuals. Differing standards of value affect the way we understand words, too. For example, your "beautiful modern art" may be a "ridiculous object" or a "blob of paint" to me—or vice versa.

Humor may confuse, but humor *power* can improve communication and clarify our meanings. Here's another "let's suppose" illustration, from the viewpoint of Gene R.

In a friendly conversation or discussion, Gene R. may find

that another individual is totally opposed to his ideas. Gene
wants to change the other's mind. He could tell him, "You're
stubborn, stupid, and wrong." But the only thing Gene would
give or gain would be resentment.

Gene could attempt to use humor in this situation by saying, "The way I react to you is, *you're* pigheaded, thick-
headed, and wrong-headed. And those are your good points!"
But communication would still be blocked.

When Gene applies humor power, he will say, "I can see
you think *I'm* pigheaded, thick-headed, and wrong-headed.
And those are my good points!" He may not change another's
mind immediately, but he will have opened up the possibility
of change.

Alert: Remember, communication via humor power also
moves from others to us! Our listening power can increase our
humor power, for a real humorist is an individual who can
laugh at the jokes and funny sayings of others, not one who
waits impatiently to tell his joke. As Jack Frazier, a successful
manufacturer, expressed this, "A fish dies from an open
mouth." And Christopher Morley, a noted humorist, once said,
"You make the jokes—and I see them."

Let's use our humor power to understand each other.

Laugh with the Big Ones

I was there when the president of a large firm, who had been
having some minor but well-publicized differences with the In-
ternal Revenue Service, was introduced to an audience in this
manner:

"Our next speaker needs no introduction, but he does
need a good tax attorney."

The audience roared. And so did the president.

By laughing with him, the introducer humanized that corporate executive's image. When the executive laughed, too, he
broadened the channels of communication. *Before* he laughed
at himself, people in the audience probably believed, "Ha! He

thinks he's a big shot." *After* he laughed, their feelings surely changed to, "Aha! He's human, after all."

The need to humanize one's personal image is a psychological and sociological concept understood by high-level achievers in every field. It's a concept applied by leaders in business, industry, education, politics, religion, sports, the arts —including the art of living! Leaders know this:

Each of us is divided from others by our frames of reference, life-styles, and experiences. Yet all of us are linked by our need for understanding and acceptance. If we can bring forth our human qualities, others can identify with and accept us.

Humor power recognizes the human factor. Thus the truly great laugh at themselves and encourage others to laugh with them. They give and gain by sharing their humanity. And so can you!

Sammy Davis, Jr., has laughed at himself through the story of a bus driver who demanded, "Move to the back of the bus."

Said Davis, "I'll have you know I'm Jewish."

"Okay," responded the driver, "then get off the bus."

Paul Lynde, of TV's "Hollywood Squares," didn't like his father's profession. So he told people his father was a cattle surgeon, not a butcher.

Many famous people, performers in particular, have made laughing at themselves a communications asset. They capitalized on the humor of a conventionally unattractive feature. Martha Raye's big mouth, for example, or Jimmy Durante's "schnozzola."

Or, they laughed at a farcical "fact," usually invented, about themselves. Jack Benny was tight with money, and Dean Martin is always tight.

As radio greats, Benny and Fred Allen communicated with their listeners by carrying on a fake feud. Insisting that Jack's humor was prepackaged for him by gag writers, Fred quipped, "Jack Benny couldn't ad-lib a belch after a Hungarian dinner."

Abe Lincoln laughed at himself, and especially at his appearance. He opened up communication by telling this story:

"Sometimes I feel like the ugly man who met an old woman traveling through a forest.

"The old woman said, 'You're the ugliest man I ever saw.'

" 'I can't help it,' the ugly man said.

" 'No, I guess not,' the woman admitted, 'but the least you could do is stay at home.' "

Two-Faced?

Accused by Stephen A. Douglas of being two-faced, Lincoln protested. Anyone should know, he said, that he couldn't have two faces.

"If I had," he declared, "I wouldn't wear this one!"

From another approach, there's:

Woody's Way

"I wasn't a good-looking kid," humorist Woody Allen has said. "I didn't acquire these looks until later in life."

Humorist Bob Hope has often communicated by laughing at his golf game. He once said, "If you watch a game, it's fun. If you play it, it's recreation. If you work at it, it's golf." And, at an Arnold Palmer roast, "I wear Arnold Palmer shirts, Arnold Palmer shoes, Arnold Palmer pants, but—I play golf like Betsy Palmer."

Laughing at the way you look, or at something you've done not too gracefully, humanizes you. If you happen to be handsome or beautiful, thanks to the accident of ancestry, your good looks may awe others. Put people at ease. Play up another flaw!

For yourself, remember the bumper sticker "Stamp Out Conceit. You'll Love Yourself for It."

If you don't have a funny flaw, invent one! But faults are usually easy to find.

Consider the college football coach who was asked about a star player. The coach said, "He's a senior. He's great, but he has one fault. He's a senior."

If your traits, abilities, or achievements might arouse envy or even fear, try to change those negative responses. For instance, you could quip, "Nobody's perfect. And I'm the perfect example!" Your self-directed and shared laughter will help others like, respect, and admire you—because your humor power shows you're human, too.

"I like you" leads to "I understand you" and on to "I believe you." Then, the goal you reach is trust. When others trust you, you'll influence them to motivate themselves and develop their full potential. And that's the ultimate aim of every communicator and motivator.

Achieve a WINNING Attitude

Your winning attitude comes from thinking affirmatively—and realistically. Psychologists have called this "self-actualization." It means, realize what is possible and, if necessary, adjust your goals. At first, this may seem to be a narrow, limiting concept. But psychologists also believe that self-actualization demands the development of all the abilities and potential you possess. And that's a big goal!

Instead of aiming for the blue sky, try to reach for the possible. Seek to define your goals, not in large, general terms, but in terms you can visualize. See the beginning, if not the end, of your journey. If you never do less than your best, you'll certainly be a winner!

You'll recognize a winning attitude when you can tell the difference between having a failure and being one. Losers think one failure means it's time to give up. Winners know that a failure is a temporary setback. They accept the challenge to get up and try again.

What's more, your winning attitude will flourish with help from humor power. It will help you be realistic without becoming discouraged. And it will help you overcome bad odds and difficulties. Why not survey the power of humor from the vantage point of these two anecdotes:

Famous football coach Knute Rockne won, and helped his players win, with humor power.

On one occasion, Knute's Notre Dame football team was behind Wisconsin 7–0 at half time. In the locker room, he was silent until time to return to the field. Then he shouted, "All right, girls, let's go."

Knute Rockne's winning attitude was, "We're all in this together, so let's share a laugh." With humor power, he sparked courage and helped his players forget the odds were against them. What's more, his humor power helped overcome the odds. The Notre Dame team played on to victory.

When you apply humor power, you can spark courage in others, inspire them to triumph over difficulty—and enjoy personal success.

Comedian Joe Frisco, once asked about his motivation to think and be funny onstage and off, explained, "I stutter. And I was afraid that if I didn't have something funny to say, people wouldn't wait till I got to the end of a sentence."

Frisco succeeded as a comedian and as an individual, thanks to his ability to take his handicap lightly. We can be more successful, too, if we refuse to take our flaws too seriously.

How Stevenson Succeeded

Twice defeated by Dwight D. Eisenhower in presidential elections, Adlai Stevenson never lost the winning attitude of humor power.

Acknowledging the honor of his first presidential nomination, he admitted he was flattered, quipping, "I suppose flattery hurts no one. That is, if he doesn't inhale."

The morning after the first loss to Eisenhower, he greeted reporters at his door with the humor-powered invitation "Come in and have some fried postmortems on toast."

Some years later, Stevenson was the featured speaker at a luncheon. He arrived late, delayed by an armed forces parade.

He apologized, explaining, "Military heroes are always getting in my way."

Stevenson changed his image from loser to winner and became memorable. Let's change our image with humor power!

GAIN WITHOUT GLOATING

When we do win, we'll win bigger if we don't get too excited about our success. Remember, we didn't do it alone. And there is always someone behind us, pushing us onward to achieve— even if it's only a bill collector.

Humor power helps make our modesty believable. And we can gain by taking ourselves lightly—as these examples suggest:

How to Be a Hero

President John F. Kennedy was asked how he became a hero in World War II.

"I couldn't help it," he replied. "The Japanese sank my boat."

What Makes a Star?

TV celebrity Johnny Carson was asked, "What makes you a star?"

He answered, with the self-directed laughter of humor power, "I started out in a gaseous state, and then I cooled."

No-Talent Winner

Humorous writer Robert Benchley confessed that it took him fifteen years to discover he had no talent for writing.

"Then it was too late," he said. "I couldn't give up writing because I was too famous."

While it's wise to be modest, winners don't belittle themselves. They maintain their self-esteem, recognize their winning worth, and accept it. Let me illustrate this by comparing two versions of the same story.

The first version shows how humor power helps us gain without gloating and with modesty.

A new man joined the company team, and an associate introduced their boss. "This is Jerry, our president," the associate said, then joked, "He's a natural-born leader— son of the owner." And all three shared a laugh.

Humor power helped to humanize Jerry without deflating his pride. By laughing, he showed he could think lightly about his status.

From the second version, we can learn why humor power helps us assert our winning worth without being too modest.

Another new-on-the-job executive met his boss, the president, in a similar situation. And this executive joked, "Well, Ralph, I suppose you're a natural-born leader—son of the owner."

"No," Ralph replied, lightly but seriously, "I'm the great-grandson of the founder."

Although Ralph didn't gloat, he gently implied that he had reached success through his own efforts and proudly carried on a family tradition.

We affirm our winning worth when we take ourselves lightly and our roles in life seriously.

Be EFFECTIVE,
Not Only Efficient

Today, we all stress the importance of being efficient in our personal, family, and on-the-job roles. We want to get organized, although "well-organized, structured" often means "static, not moving." We want to be efficient because we think we can save time and set ourselves free to enjoy life more. But we may get exactly the opposite result if all we achieve is efficiency. I believe humor power can help us be effective as well. Then we'll really use our time instead of just saving it!

For example, if we make a point of being on time for meetings or meals, we're efficient. But if we concentrate on routine without really saying anything at the meeting or the meal, we are not effective. In fact, efficient attention to detail can cause others to give us yes answers when they actually mean no—or worse. At a meeting, yes may mean: "I wonder what he's driving at?"; "Wow, what a bore he is!"; "If this meeting doesn't break up soon, I'll miss my lunch date"; or a variety of other thoughts that block achievement. Let's try, instead, for effectiveness!

Whether you lead the meeting, initiate a conversation at dinner, or seek to communicate in any situation of your personal and professional life, humor power can help you humanize yourself, inspire others, and be effective. You can stimulate helpful, and therefore affirmative, discussion in place of an empty yes. And you can begin by thinking funny.

In a business situation, for instance, you can be more effective when you state a problem humorously and then suggest a serious solution. Your think-funny remark might be, "Our business really isn't a nonprofit organization; it just seems that way," or, "Doing business today is like Mickey Rooney dancing with Raquel Welch. The overhead is fantastic."

Thinking funny stems from your feelings and your manner as well as your words. With feeling, you can open an emotional outlet for others and help them feel better about themselves. You might do this by using a one-liner that humanizes a mistake—any mistake—you made: "I always suspected I could be brainwashed with an eyedropper."

From the perspective of putting yourself and your humanity into situations and problems, thinking funny is more effective than being funny. However, others may interpret your way of thinking funny as a means of being funny. What happens then?

If other individuals react only to the being-funny surface level of your humor power, they can still gain a lot through light relief from momentary stresses. And your humor power will not fail, because you will know it gave help to others.

In addition, you can employ humor for the power to smooth out conflicts in human relationships. With a little bit of humor—a story, vignette, aphorism, or one-liner—you can kid people into doing things or accepting things they wouldn't do or accept otherwise.

Rule!

If you want to rule the world, you must keep it amused.

—RALPH WALDO EMERSON

You're amusing when you advise young men to buy Girl Scout Cookies because "today's Brownie is tomorrow's cupcake." You add effectiveness to amusement when you say, "A man can't have his cake and someone else's cookie, too. Or he'll wind up in a crummy situation." Here, your humor power is effective because it gently reminds others that greed can create "a crummy situation" by entangling individuals in problems.

When you want to determine the effectiveness of your humor power, measure it in terms of when and why you use it. A lot of your humor power will depend on the reasons you have for applying it, the emotions you have as you apply it, and the way you apply it to put others in the mood for accepting you and your ideas.

Day by day, every humor-power situation is composed of unpleasant experiences playfully enjoyed combined with pleasant experiences in varying degrees and proportions. Anything that might be unpleasant if taken seriously, together with anything that might for any reason be accepted as pleasant, can constitute validity for the creation of humor power.

But if humor is to be effective, others need to experience a playfulness as they respond. Humor power enables us to put others in a playful mood. An example from a famous humorist can show us how.

Browsing through the library of a neighbor, Mark Twain found a book that appealed to him. He asked if he could borrow it.

"You're welcome to read it anytime, if you read it here," the neighbor said, and explained, "You see, I have a rule that books cannot leave these premises."

A few weeks later, the neighbor called on Twain and asked to borrow his lawn mower. "Certainly," said Twain, "but according to my rule, you must use it on these premises."

Like Twain, we usually need a playful approach if we would change others' attitudes. It's more difficult—but it *is* possible—to influence others through the use of hostile humor.

When hostile humor isn't really hostile

In my estimation, we can sometimes apply hostile humor playfully and effectively—because humor that may seem hostile really isn't when we put ourselves into it. Then we can do what educators and psychologists call "acting out" instead of "acting on."

You don't have to be in show business to "act out." You're onstage anywhere, anytime. You can act out and alleviate your problems, resentments, anguish, and embarrassment. Importantly, you'll aid others by showing them how to act out their troubles.

Paradoxically, hostile humor can offer a kind of caring, affection, and tenderness—when it's converted to humor power. An example I use to illustrate this concerns the man who appears at his neighbor's door, hatchet in hand, saying, "I've come to fix your stereo set."

As long as he doesn't chop up the stereo, this man is acting out his irritation at the noise from the set, not acting on anger at his neighbor. And he's giving a kind of affection. His acting out tells the neighbor, "I like you, I care about you, and I want to get along with you. So won't you please turn down the stereo?"

You don't need a prop, such as a hatchet, to act out. Try putting yourself and your feelings into your humor—for humor power.

In fact, another paradox of humor power suggests that we can effectively employ humor that seems hostile only when we use it with or about someone we love. This kind of humor might be called disparaging or denigrating instead of hostile. Frequently, it appears, denigrating humor is applied to women. For example:

Corporate executives sometimes joke about their wives' extravagance, saying, "My wife couldn't keep money in her handbag if it were lined with flypaper," or "My wife told me, 'I admit I like to spend money. But name one other extravagance I have.'"

On the surface, such jokes may seem disparaging. But another interpretation is that these executives love their wives, are really proud of them, and think they are more attractive and better-dressed than other women in their social or business group. The executives kid their wives' supposed extravagance as a way to avoid boasting and to act out their love and pride.

In my own case, the same interpretation applies. My wife, Betty Ann, is financial manager and secretary-treasurer of our TEAM, so any joke I may tell about her methods of managing money is clearly not factual or denigrating but illustrates the truth that this kind of humor gains a different, deeper meaning when we use it with or about those we love.

Certainly, I'm not advocating the constant or increased

use of disparaging humor. But I suggest that such humor can be transformed into humor power to help us act out our warm feelings, too.

Insulate, and Unload

Acting out helps us to insulate ourselves and others against the explosive potential of highly charged subjects. As we act out our feelings on those subjects, we can unload tensions without evoking resentment.

When you and a friend or colleague can't agree about a controversial subject, you and he have three psychological options: (1) agree to disagree, (2) modify your opinions and compromise, or (3) never speak to each other again! With the light touch of humor power, you can cancel number three and exercise either of the first two options.

What's more, humor power can protect your own ego while it prevents you from antagonizing others. You can be more effective in talking about things you wouldn't ordinarily talk about to certain persons and groups.

Insulate, and unload! For instance, if the topic is sex education, you might quote a quip from a veterinarian. When he was asked why there are more rabbits than squirrels, the veterinarian answered, "Did you ever try to make love in a tree?"

Or you might declare, "Our children should learn about sex the way we did—off the rest-room walls." This satirical one-liner can help others understand and perhaps accept your unspoken words: "Sex education could be better than misinformation about sex."

Soothe, Don't Scratch

Satire can be effective in getting people to listen to you and remember what you say. It can wake up a conversation, flag and hold a listener's attention, and communicate ideas.

During His sojourn on earth, Jesus Christ used satire's power to communicate His messages. When He inquired,

"Would one of you hand his son a stone when he asks for a loaf?" the satirical shock equaled this modern question: "If your kid wanted a peanut-butter sandwich, would you hit him with a rock?"

Christ compared the act of asking for a loaf to the need of His listeners for help from their heavenly Father, and His message was: "Ask and you will receive."

Alert: Remember, satire needs to be handled with care. It's more intellectual than thumbing one's nose, but it's also closer to cruelty. And, even more than satire, sarcastic insults can plunge dangerously deep into others' anxieties.

Some seasoned professionals have used insults effectively. For instance, Groucho Marx called Texans "damn Yankees." He made them love it and laugh, for Groucho was master of the insult.

Even in the mouths of professionals, sarcasm may not work. Comedian Mort Sahl's humor bombed with some audiences when he "joked," "Leon Jaworski tells me I'm still grieving about Jack Kennedy's death. Well, he's still dead, isn't he?" Less bitter, but still biting, was Oscar Levant's remark: "My doctor won't allow me to watch Dinah Shore. I'm a diabetic."

Abe Lincoln knew how to be satirical. Impatient with General George B. McClellan for not following up military advantages, he wrote this letter:

My dear McClellan:
    If you don't want to use the army, I should like to borrow it for a while.

Yours respectfully,
A. Lincoln

Apparently, Lincoln had second thoughts. He didn't mail that letter! And in general he preferred to express compassion instead of applying satire. This familiar example shows his compassionate, humor-powered nature: Defending a soldier who deserted his post, he said to his military leaders, "I put it to you to decide for yourselves. If Almighty God gives a man a cowardly pair of legs, how can he help their running away with him?"

Satire does have a place. Primarily, it's needed to expose the shams of institutions and beliefs that can damage us. If we are to use it, I believe it calls for two things. First, we need to feel at home with our satirical humor power. We must know that it's relevant and will meet with recognition. Second, we must be sure that our target—individual or group—can see the funny side and will think funny about our satire.

With practice, we can learn to use satire effectively. But compassionate humor is almost always more effective in daily life. Let's follow Lincoln's example, and employ humor power to smooth, not scratch.

When we deal with touchy subjects—politics, sex, religion, for example—we can soothe and smooth by focusing humor power on ourselves. Perhaps the best way I can demonstrate this is by giving you some examples from my personal and professional experiences.

My TEAM associates say that "Herb has made presentations to meat packers, pickle packers, chicken pluckers, plasterers, and the plastered. He has spoken to dieticians in Hawaii, to Russian humorists in Moscow, and to Texans in vain." The way they tell it, I've spoken to every kind of group—except Democrats, who wouldn't listen to me.

During Democratic administrations, I always admit I'm still a Republican. Very still. Actually, I try to give equal time to the two major parties. If I say, "When trouble comes, donkeys form a circle and kick each other," I also say, "They're trying to cross an elephant with a winner, but they keep getting Dumbo." My goal is to have the humility to laugh at Republican mistakes. Too.

In fact, I hope people will play down my honors and play up my humility. And they do. They don't call me "your speaker, Dr. Herb True." They call me "that fellow with all those kids." Five jacks—three queens.

Some years ago, I met a friend while I was shopping. "My wife and I are celebrating," I said to him. "I want to get her a bottle of perfume."

"What are you celebrating?" he asked.

"The birth of our eighth child," I replied.

"Look," my friend told me, "your wife doesn't need perfume. She needs a repellent."

Often, I test my humor power by trying it out on friends and colleagues. When I tell a weather vignette, in personal or professional life, it may tie in with religion. For example: "After an earthquake, I was asked how long it had lasted. I answered, 'Exactly fourteen Hail Marys.'"

Perhaps the worst thing that can be said about humor power is that, by putting us in a good mood, it enables us to tolerate ourselves. The best thing is that it enables us to tolerate each other. Even if we cannot worship together, accept the same beliefs, or approve the same ideas, we can share our humor power more often.

Alert: Although humor power can help us treat delicate subjects lightly, ethnic humor is almost too delicate to handle. The risk of offending others is great, and the chance of gaining anything is remote indeed. An exception may be: When you and everyone else in a group share the same heritage, ethnic humor may lighten the burdens of all. But even then, there's a high-risk factor, because groups are made up of individuals. And what amuses one individual may be perceived by another as an insult.

Once again, I can best illustrate this with a personal experience. As I visited with a friend, I opened our conversation by saying, "Let me tell you a new Polish joke."

"Stop right there, Herb," my friend said. "I don't want to hear it."

"I don't understand," I protested. "You're Polish-American, and part of my heritage is Polish-American, too. Why can't we share a Polish joke?"

"Forget it," my friend insisted. "Don't tell me any Polish jokes."

His warning signals reached me, and I changed the subject.

Soothe, don't scratch! Each of us can focus humor power on ourselves. Then we'll become memorable for our ability to relate to others.

Reap Rewarding RESULTS

Humor power rewards you with greater self-knowledge, especially if you've ever had a secret feeling that humor isn't dignified. It renews your self-confidence, releases your freedom to be yourself, and results in an improved ability to cope with everyday downs and ups. What's more, humor power helps you seize the day, laughing in the present without brooding over the woes and worries of the past.

Satchel Paige, the great pitcher, spent long years in the Negro leagues before he joined the pitching staff of the American League's Cleveland Indians. Wasting no time on regrets, he dedicated himself to the serious job of winning games, and a pennant, while taking himself lightly. He succeeded.

Satch Said It

Don't look back. Somebody may be catching up.

—SATCHEL PAIGE

A fresh perspective of yourself and others, the opportunity to communicate by opening up, a better approach to winning, and the ability to be effective as well as efficient are basic, helpful concepts. It's my belief that humor power can help you turn these concepts into valuable realities, draw on your inner resources—and gain rewards.

TRUE THOUGHTS ABOUT HUMOR

Help yourself to a new	P	erspective
Use your	O	pportunity to communicate
Make your attitude a	W	inning one
Over-all, be	E	ffective, not just efficient
Reach up to rewarding	R	esults

Important rewards result from humor power in your personal life, in your marriage and family life, and on the job. Look ahead—to your personal humor power!

4   Humor Power in Your Personal Life

Humor power, I suggest, won't make you tall when you're short or thin when you're fat. It won't pay your bills or do your work for you. It won't make people fall in love with you at first sight, and it cannot always make you happy when you're sad.

But it can help! If you think funny and take yourself lightly, you'll find it easier to accept your height, weight, and other physical attributes for what they are: a part of you, but not nearly as important as the way you feel about yourself. You'll find that humor power helps you see financial worries in perspective: a problem you can feel better about as you work to overcome it.

Although you may not gain instant love, you can warm up your personal relationships—by sharing laughter. Even a casual encounter with a person you may never see again becomes more rewarding, thanks to shared laughter. You might think of the casually met person as your neighbor, and then consider this:

"You simply must learn that if you can interest the neighbor, you can interest all the neighbors, or the world, and not be frozen by magnitudes," wrote psychologist Daniel W. Josselyn.

Sharing laughter helps you interest your neighbors! It can help you identify with your neighbors' problems and worries, especially when the laugh you share is focused on yourself. Many little worries tend to grow into big anxieties—until you view them from the perspective of self-focused laughter. Then you can show others it's all right to think funny about the human frailties that magnify little worries.

What's more, your neighbors will help you become a more tender, more tolerant individual. As they laugh at themselves and with you, they'll help you see yourself—and open up.

Yes, all of the above is a lot for humor power to do! But, day by day, this power *can* help you lift the load of problems large and small. Let me suggest some ways to begin.

MINIMIZE Minor Matters

Laugh about the little things in daily life that irritate all of us and watch irritations vanish. By sharing laughter, you can put trivial problems in their proper place and in proportion to the whole of life. You'll remind others that it helps to take some things lightly, and you'll lift their spirits.

Do something about the weather. Laugh at it!

"Probably the last fully accurate weather forecast was when God told Noah there was a hundred per cent chance of precipitation."

Weather jokes, I find, lift the spirits of my audiences on days when it's too wet, too hot, or too cold. In your personal life, try some of these spirit-lifters:

"Weather forecasters predicted a heavy dew. This morning, my neighbor stepped off his front porch. Now they're dragging the dew for his body."

"Sure, we have air conditioning. I've never seen air in such condition."

"It got so cold in my office, my desk chair had snow tires."

"If we have another bad winter, I'm going to retire. I'll

strap a snow shovel on top of my car and head south. I won't
stop till someone points to the shovel and says, 'What's that
thing for?' "

Think funny about wet or dry weather and try telling this
story:

Talking with a sun-tanned resident, a visitor to New Mexico asked, "Don't you ever get any rain here?"

The resident thought, then asked, "Do you remember the
story about Noah and the ark, and how it rained for forty days
and forty nights?"

"Of course I remember that story," said the visitor.

"That time," declared the New Mexican, "we got about an
inch."

Smile and share, while you wait. You're in the slow line at
the supermarket check-out or at the bank. Fidget, like everyone else. Or, share your humor power!

"It's nature's law. The other line moves faster."

"Speed isn't everything. If it were, rabbits would rule the
world."

And only at the supermarket: "I started out with three
flounders. But I've been in this line so long, now I have one
flounder and two smelt."

Kid yourself about your golf game. Or, bowling, fishing,
tennis, boating, bridge—whatever pastime enlivens your leisure
life. You might say, "The trouble with leisure is, someone is
always trying to steal mine." Or, "Political campaigns have
taught us that not all persons who stretch the facts are fisher-
men and golfers."

Once again, your humor power can create a better climate
for others and improve your own personal atmosphere or self-
image. Lightly, you imply that all of us are lucky when we're
able to enjoy leisure pastimes. It's your way of saying, "Little
things can make us happy."

If you are a golfer, you can tell people you shoot in the
low seventies, because if it gets any colder, you don't play!
Thus you suggest that it doesn't seriously bother you when
your score is higher than you'd like it to be, for golfing helps

you to relax. And thinking funny about golf also relaxes you. To help your neighbors identify with this viewpoint, you can experiment with other quips and vignettes.

Golf-Offs

A golfer asked his caddy, "How do you like my game?" "It's okay," said the caddy, "but I like golf better."

"My wife ran over my golf clubs," one golfer claimed. "Well, she did tell me not to leave them on the porch."

St. Peter led off with a hole in one. St. Thomas followed with a hole in one. St. Andrew said, "All right, now let's cut out the miracles and play golf."

"I'm glad it's spring," declared the golfer. "I'd much rather swear at a golf ball than a snow shovel."

"Show me a good loser, and I'll show you a man who is playing golf with his boss."

"My doctor said I can't play golf," a golfer remarked. And his partner answered, "Oh, he's played with you, too."

Nothing increases your golf score like witnesses!

Golf pro Jack Nicklaus once asked baseball pro Henry Aaron, "What kind of golfer are you?"

"It took me seventeen years to get three thousand hits in baseball," Aaron answered. "I did it in one afternoon on the golf course."

More than any other game, it seems, golf provokes the humor-powered to think funny. Hundreds, perhaps thousands, of quips, stories, and anecdotes about golf exist. Other games do have their humor-powered moments. Observe this bridge-table bungle.

"On just what did you bid one no-trump?" a wife asked. "*I* had four aces and three kings."

"Truthfully, dear," replied her husband, "I bid it on one queen, two jacks, three martinis, and wine with dinner."

Show yourself as you are. Openness with others helps us admit that we sometimes feel insecure or doubtful about ourselves. Through humor power, we can admit insecurities without being too serious. Then we can erase doubts, strengthen our self-image, and firm up the common ground of shared humanity. And we needn't worry about being too open. We can be confident that our flaws, our background, and our circumstances, past or present, are better by far than any evasions we might use to hide them.

Have you ever felt tempted to apologize for, or brag about, your family background?

Consider the driver who told a highway patrolman, "I'll have you know I come from one of the best families in Virginia. You can't give me a ticket."

"That's okay," said the patrolman. "We aren't ticketing you for breeding purposes."

Or the two persons who compared ancestral notes:

One said, "My family dates back to King John of England."

"Sorry," the other apologized. "Mine lost all their records in the great flood."

Or the late Everett Dirksen, Illinois Senator:

When Ev first ran for Congress, he listened to an opponent hold forth about his family. The opponent's grandfather had been a general, and his uncle, a judge on the state supreme court. It was Ev's turn to speak.

"Ladies and gentlemen," he began, "it has been my great privilege to be descended from a long line—of married folks."

Born, Not Made

Poet Rod McKuen once joked about the fact that he was born out of wedlock. "I was born a bastard," McKuen said. "It takes some people all their lives to become one."

Perhaps you think you live, or lived, on the wrong side of the tracks, the town, or the suburb? Or you feel embarrassed about financial circumstances of the past? Here are some ways the humor-powered have coped with those minor embarrassments. Create your own ways, and use them!

"I'll tell you what kind of neighborhood I grew up in. When a garage mechanic said your engine was missing, he meant your engine was missing."

"We were never poor, never went hungry, but we put off some meals indefinitely."

"I come from a very poor family. When I was a kid, other children made model airplanes. I made model hamburgers."

What Money Can't Buy

Speaking of her early Brooklyn years, Barbra Streisand kidded, "We were awful poor. But we had a lot of things money can't buy. Like unpaid bills."

Do you think you have too much education, or too little? Or do you feel that your honors or achievements may give others the image of you as puffed up and self-important? If you can kid yourself, you won't overawe others or take your role in life too lightly.

Great achievers have shown us how to put honors and rewards in perspective. You might apply these examples to your personal life:

Taking Honors Lightly

Famous, successful, and colorful Supreme Court Justice Oliver Wendell Holmes took himself lightly. He wasn't pompous or puffed up about his many honors.

When a young woman came to Washington to see the Justice's sculptured likeness unveiled, she was overwhelmed to meet the famous man in person. "I've traveled four hundred miles to see your bust unveiled!" she exclaimed.

Replied the Justice, "Gladly would I travel four hundred miles to return the compliment."

When Lincoln was asked how he liked being President, he replied, "You've heard the story of the man who was tarred and feathered and ridden out of town on a rail.

"Someone wanted to know how he liked it, and he said, 'If it wasn't for the honor of the thing, I'd rather walk.' "

That example inspires me, and helps me remember that life is one long lesson in humility. As a research psychologist, I hope to teach by sharing my feelings about humility and other emotions. In my personal and professional life, "egghead" isn't the image I have of myself. But the image created by my post-graduate degrees may block person-to-person or person-to-audience communication.

So I ask my introducers to kid me. And I try to show that, although I take my job in life very seriously, I think lightly about myself. For instance, I might say, "Sure, I have degrees. But don't let that shake you up. Thermometers have degrees, too."

When humor power helps us open up emotionally, we and the people around us feel better. In addition, humor power can help us feel better physically.

HELP YOURSELF
TO HEALTH

Yes, humor power can improve your health. Laughter, for example, is easy, pleasant exercise. Modern medical science tells us laughter benefits the heart, compensates for low and high blood pressure, improves digestion, enhances survival, and prolongs life.

These medical views are backed up by objective studies of laughter's effect. At Northwestern University, a study conducted under strict, scientific test conditions demonstrated this: The act of laughing massages the heart, stimulates blood circulation, and helps the lungs breathe easier. Another test, at Fordham University, reinforced the conclusion that laughter benefits the heart, lungs, stomach, and other organs. It relaxes our tensions and promotes a feeling of physical well-being.

From the Bible, from mankind's past history, and from our instincts, we learn that humor power can be applied to improve our health. Many of Solomon's proverbs tell us humor and health go together. For example, one proverb reminds us that joy in the heart equals health for the body. Ancient Romans believed that laughter belonged at the banquet table, because it improved digestion. And, after we enjoy a good laugh, we often say, intuitively, "I really needed that."

What's more, the power of humor can help you and others feel better—about your hospital stay, illness, or accident. New Yorker Miriam Tormey proved that. She slipped on the winter ice, broke her left arm, and, even more painfully, dislocated her shoulder. With a smile, she told friends, "If you have a choice, don't dislocate a shoulder. Break an arm!"

When the sick visit you, or vice versa, you can cheer them up with health-related stories and one-liners from fact or fiction.

A visitor knocked on the door of Dorothy Parker's hospital room. She called out, "Who goes there, friend or enema?"

"I don't have much faith in my doctor," an invalid complained. "All his patients are sick."

Dialogue: "I've been seeing spots in front of my eyes." "Have you seen a doctor?" "No, just spots."

Another dialogue: "How do you want your medicine today?"

"With a fork."

"Did you know that space scientists are asking physicians and surgeons for help? They want hints on how to soar higher into space, like medical/surgical fees."

Doug told his doctor, "I've been misbehaving, Doc, and my conscience is bothering me."

"You want something to make your willpower stronger," the doctor deduced.

"Actually," Doug said, "I'm more interested in something to weaken my conscience."

And Charlie, who had a swinging reputation, went to his doctor for a physical checkup. As he put his shirt back on, he asked, "Well, Doc, do I have to give up wine, women, and song?"

"Not exactly, Charlie," said the doctor. "You can sing all you want to."

Alert: Use healthy, happy humor power to heal, not hurt. Misguided humor may upset others' emotional well-being and injure you, in their eyes.

Turn Off Tensions

When we apply our humor power to the tensions and anxieties that beset us in our personal lives, we can help ourselves, and others. The serious problems of society—energy, inflation, crime, for example—seem to magnify our little problems. We may feel pressured to succeed financially, and we wonder whether we can. Or, we may be plagued by worries about our personal appearance or our age. At the same time, we probably feel that the world cares too much about money and appearances, and too little about us as individuals.

Humor power helps us to realize that some of our anxieties are absurd in relation to larger problems. If we can show that we take our little worries lightly, others will identify with us and care more about us. But our biggest gain will come when we can identify with others and care more about them—because one of the strongest of all human longings is the need to be needed.

With humor power, you can turn off tensions and relieve worries about everything from age to weight to money. For instance, aging seems to be the worry that's hardest for most people to handle. No matter how young or how old you are, you can help others think lightly about aging. Here's a humor-powered example:

Minus Is Plus

Speaker Cavett Robert of Phoenix is noted for his youthful spirit of fun and play. What's more, he signed a five-year speaking contract—on his seventieth birthday.

In his personal and public life, he takes his age lightly—and turns a minus into a plus. "I want to die young as late as possible," Cavett says.

In your personal life, you'll discover that humor has power to identify age as an emotional, more than a biological, state.

Which of these humor-power applications fits you? Or comes closest?

"He's in the awkward age—the twenties. Too old to be a child prodigy but too young to play a teen-ager on a TV show."

"Middle age is the time when 'getting ahead' begins to mean 'staying even.'"

"Some senior citizens have the ability to laugh when friends make a donation to a retirement home in their honor. A year's supply of prune juice."

"I'm so old, my insurance company sent me half a calendar."

Humor-powered people know how to laugh at any age.

"I've discovered the secret of eternal youth," Bob Hope once quipped. "I lie about my age."

A woman—call her Helen—took a different approach. "I never lie about my age," Helen insisted. "I lie about my husband's age. Then I tell the truth. I'm younger than he is."

"Our daughter Lisa is fifteen going on eighteen," I said—when she was. "That seems to be the awkward age. She knows how to make a phone call, but doesn't know how to end one."

"I don't mind growing older," a wise man said. "I don't even mind showing my age, just as long as I don't have to like the way it makes me look."

You're worried about falling, or failed, hair? I empathize! But the best cure for baldness is still a hat.

Or, put it another way: "Hair is the only thing that will prevent baldness."

Remember: "Being bald has advantages. You're the first one to know when it starts to rain."

"About this hairpiece I saw advertised," said a man whose hair was going, "I want to get one. The ad said you're able to go boating, golfing, skiing, swimming. That would be great! I can't do all those things now."

Do you worry about your weight? Spare a thought for the

man who fretted, "I've been trying to diet for six months, and the only thing that's getting thin is my hair."

Weigh in with humor power! Fat and how to lose it is one of today's most popular topics—equaled only by discussions of diets and how to follow them. Why complain, when you can quip?

"One of the most perplexing issues of our time is, where does weight go when we lose it?"

"I'm on such a strict diet, I can't even listen to dinner music."

"My doctor put me on a no-starch diet. I can eat all the soap and bleach I want."

"We're going through an identity crisis. Most Americans are trying to find out who they are, what they're made of, and how they can lose ten or twenty pounds of it."

Personal worries about our role in life will evaporate when we heed the words humor-powered winners use to prevent self-importance.

Self-Made

I'm a self-made man. But I think if I had it to do over again, I'd call in someone else.

—ROLAND YOUNG

Foil Financial Worries

No doubt about it. Money matters! But it matters much less when you invest your humor power in taking everyday money problems lightly. Put big-money goals in perspective.

Big Money Blues

Successful playwright George S. Kaufman had ten thousand dollars. Back in the twenties, that was big money. He also had friends—among them, the comic Marx brothers.

The brothers recommended stocks, and Kaufman invested. His ten thousand disappeared in the stock market crash of 1929.

He was philosophical. "Anybody who takes the Marx brothers' advice about investing money," he said, "deserves to lose it."

Do yourself a favor! Let humor power help you think small about financial woes, and encourage others to do the same.

Tell your neighbor, "Let's make a deal. I'll stop keeping up with you, if you'll stop keeping up with me."

You might say, of someone else, "He's so loaded, he has bookends for his bankbooks."

About yourself, you might remark, "I've figured out what's wrong. My tastes are in the tennis bracket, but I get Ping-Pong pay."

Or, be philosophical with: "Today, the only place ends meet is on the football field."

Let a humor-powered perspective relieve the pain when cash shortages pinch. Face up to financial facts with: "About the only thing you can do on a shoestring is trip."

Or, you could lighten the load by telling this story about one man's way to . . .

Think Funny About Money

An insurance man was teaching his wife to drive. As the car headed downhill, the brakes failed.

"I can't stop!" the wife screamed. "What do I do now?"

"Pray," he instructed, "and try to hit something cheap."

If you want to kid about your financial success, you might say, "A wonderful thing about money is, it goes with any outfit you wear."

Or, if you want to focus on the financial crunch of modern life, you could report to your friends, "Some people are starting a movement to protest high taxes. Their idea? Send a tea bag to your congressman!"

Let's hope the following never happens to you and me!

Scree-eech!

This morning, I stepped into a crosswalk without looking.

A car screeched to a halt, and the driver, smiling sweetly, said, "I brake for animals, you jackass."

—ROBERT ORBEN

Note that Bob suggested the "I" or "laugh-at-yourself" approach—just one reason why many corporate executives, entertainers, and others rely, for humor-power resources, on his *Current Comedy* newsletter, which often takes the self-directed way to humor.

In the simplest situations, your humor-powered perspective can relieve tensions. Discover chuckles in the commonplace. You could follow the example set by Henny Youngman, king of the one-liner, and take your humor power wherever you go. Getting into an elevator, he has made others laugh by saying, "Second floor, sundries, notions, ladies' lingerie. Breathe in. It's a little crowded."

On the serious side, humor power lifts burdens. You can gain the inner strength to make changes for the better—and to accept the unchangeable.

Problems of personal life plagued two-time Oscar-winner Bette Davis. She faced them with humor power, but the problems kept coming. "By the time I was fifty," she said, "I began to wonder. I thought, 'Surely I've built enough character by now?'"

In another important area of your personal life, turning off tension with humor power brings rewards.

SUCCEED IN SOCIAL LIFE

Poise. Some say it's a matter of being so stupid we don't know when we ought to be embarrassed! I like the idea that poise comes from emotional balance. It combines our power to laugh at ourselves with our genuine concern for others.

In social situations, you can gain and give poise when you see through others' eyes and then project a lighthearted view of yourself. For example:

Carol Burnett, actress and comedienne, was lunching in a restaurant when an elderly woman approached the table and lifted her hands to Carol's face.

She traced Carol's features, apologizing, "I don't see so good."

"Count your blessings," Carol said. "I don't look so good."

If we're to look good in our social lives, we need humor power. We owe it to our hosts and our fellow guests, and to our own guests. Let's hope it won't be said of us, "He was the life of the party—the only one who could talk louder than the TV set." But we can bring life to the party, by being good-humored.

Reflect your humor power in the way you enter a room. The person who sulks in, looking depressed, isn't nearly as welcome as the one who comes in smiling, looking healthy and happy.

Sound Up

Geraldine Stutz, president of Henri Bendel, New York fashion store, said it. "The most marvelous sound a guest can make is laughter."

As an element of humor power, good humor equals good manners and serves us well in social life.

Come Out of Your Shell

Be sociable, be zestful. Apply your humor power!

Break the ice, or keep it from forming, by saying something amusing. If it's the holiday season, you might ask, "Have you heard the gossip? At an IBM Christmas party, a certain computer drank a bit too much and tried to unfasten a typewriter's ribbon."

Or you might say, "At our office party, the boss's secretary told the new man in accounting he had a mind like a steel trap. He was flattered until she said, 'Stop trying to grab my leg.' "

Or: "When the head of the steno pool said we'd have a ball at Christmastime, I told her I don't dance. What she meant was, the boss is taking a Christmas-week vacation."

Or tell other guests, "I won't say this is an expensive Christmas. But we're planning to send our shopping list to the *Guinness Book of World Records* "

Whatever the season or social occasion, humor power will help you open up a conversation—and warm it up, too.

Are you going to a housewarming? Your host may be a little tense. That's your opportunity to apply a relaxing touch of humor power, by kidding him.

"When Van invited me, he told me, 'Just push the doorbell with your elbow.' I asked why I had to use my elbow, and he said, 'You're not coming empty-handed, are you?' "

(That one works for birthday and anniversary parties, too.)

Erase embarrassment. If an awkward moment occurs, take it lightly. Suppose you commit a social blunder. Remember, embarrassing situations could be worse, and often are! Try to be objective about your blunder, regain your balance, and change the subject by telling a humor-powered story.

At one party, a woman with an embarrassingly bad voice insisted on singing "My Old Kentucky Home." Head bowed, an elderly guest shed quiet tears.

Sympathetically, the hostess asked, "Are you a Kentuckian?"

"No," said the senior citizen. "I'm a musician."

Bridge the gap of embarrassment, and make a point, with another humor-powered story.

A young woman wanted to make a good impression on her fiancé's relatives at the engagement party. She entered smiling, bumped into a lamp which overturned a small table, stumbled over the table, and fell, sprawling.

She sprang to her feet, declaring, "I can do card tricks, too."

What's more, she did make a good impression. She conveyed a confident self-image by being able to laugh at herself, and, most of all, by putting others at ease. Taking ourselves lightly always works better than making a fuss!

Project yourself and your humor power into these social situations:

As she presents you to the guest of honor, your hostess whispers, "Say something flattering." But, at first glance, you're not impressed.

Say, "I can see you're the sort of person who can't be flattered."

You're introduced to another guest, who immediately stops the conversation by saying, "I've heard a lot about you."

Answer, "You can't prove a word of it."

At an important event, a friend asks, "Am I doing all right?"

Answer, "Relax—because you can't win. If you don't talk much, they'll say you're bashful. If you talk too much, they'll say you're a bore."

Your anxious hostess or host says, "I hope you're making yourself at home."

Answer, "No, I came here to get away from home."

You're dining in a large group, and the conversation becomes too heated. Cool it with "I should never argue at dinner. I'm always busy eating, so anyone who isn't hungry wins."

The neighbors asked you over for dinner and the main course proves edible—barely. It needs praising. Tell your hostess, "This tastes like a great dish I enjoyed at a French restaurant. The chef called it 'enthusiastic stew.' He put everything he had into it."

Blame your spouse. Humor-powered couples know this "secret." Husbands and wives can blame each other for social boners—arriving late, for example, at a dinner party. She took too long to dress, or he needed a road map to find his way.

It can be more effective to switch the alibis. She needed a road map to find the right outfit among the many in her closet, and he wasted time by dressing up. Or, if it's an awesomely formal event, say he put on a tie for the first time in so many months he thought he was bound to the mirror.

Draw the line. As hostess or host, and sometimes as guest, you may need to draw the line against unpleasant behavior, unreasonable demands, or uncontrolled festivity. Draw it with humor power, and avoid offending.

Stop one of those dinner-table arguments by saying, "Don't fight. You know you couldn't even lick your fingers after a chicken dinner."

To the high-spirited individual who says, "A man has to believe in something; I believe I'll have another drink," you might suggest, "Try the new cocktail called the 'pothole.' That's the one for the road."

At times, we can get the result we want only by stinging others with the half-caress of humor power. Once again, winners have shown us how.

In the book *Madame,* author Patrick O'Higgins tells about an evening when beauty-products tycoon Helena Rubenstein was entertaining friends at home. A guest repeatedly criticized her because "your ancestors burned Joan of Arc at the stake."

Embarrassed, other guests tried to change the subject, without success. Conversation grew more and more unpleasant.

At last, Helena Rubenstein said, "Well, somebody had to do it."

When a poet and a famous general were guests of honor at a dinner, their hostess tried to show—and show off—how well she knew the poet.

She announced, "My friend the poet will now compose and recite a sonnet in my honor."

"Oh, no," protested the poet. "Have the general fire a cannon."

Sting!

At a benefit dance, George Bernard Shaw partnered a self-important, but coy, woman.

As they waltzed, she fluttered, "Oh, Mr. Shaw, whatever made you ask poor little me to dance?"

Replied GBS, "This is a charity ball, isn't it?"

On one social excursion—a shopping trip to a bargain sale—tempers flared as shoppers pushed and shoved. An angry woman said to a salesclerk, "It's a good thing I'm not trying to match politeness. I'd never find it here."

Quietly, the salesclerk asked, "May I see your sample, please?"

When others are rude, it works better to show your sample of good humor.

Learn about poise from the kids. Children can teach us how to keep our social balance, with humor power.

Sometimes, our lesson comes from their view of us.

Little Jean, asked to give the blessing at a company dinner, objected, "I don't know what to say."

A guest suggested, "Say what you've heard your daddy say."

Head bent, Jean said, "My lord, where does all the money go?"

That's humor power, because Jean's honesty about Daddy's perspective can inspire us to examine our own viewpoints. And we may find that we need to balance our worries —about money, for instance—with our opportunity to enjoy ourselves in social life.

Another youngster went to a playmate's home for dinner.

His friend's mother noticed him sawing away and asked, "Do you want me to help you cut your meat?"

"Oh, no, that's all right," said little Billy. "At home, lots of times we've had meat this tough."

We can laugh with Billy. And we can also gain from this message: The way things are "at home"—in our self-directed view—may not always look the same from another's perspective. For greater social success, we may need to change our focus to the "you" direction.

Kids remind us to take our social selves lightly!

When Anne Morrow Lindbergh was a child, John D. Rockefeller came to tea. Her mother thought she might say something about Rockefeller's big nose. So, several times, Mrs. Morrow reminded her, "Please don't mention his nose."

The guest arrived. Anne greeted him politely and went off to play. Teapot in hand, the relieved Mrs. Morrow asked, "Mr. Rockefeller, will you have some cream in your nose?"

And the humor-powered thought is: If we fret because others may embarrass us, we ourselves are more likely to blunder.

Children show us it's important to communicate clearly in social life, too!

Dressed in her best, a five-year-old went to a party.

Her mother cautioned, "If the grown-ups ask you any questions about Mommy and Daddy, just tell them you don't know."

The child returned, and Mother demanded, "Did they ask you any questions?"

"Yes," said Daughter. "They wanted to know who my father is, and I told them I don't know."

As this humor-powered example shows, it's certainly better to be open with others in social situations. If we overprotect our privacy, we may communicate more than we mean.

At the Club, Wield Humor Power

Gardening, handicrafts, sports, bridge, social causes, political interests, community needs: For these and many other reasons, people gather together and form clubs. As an officer or a member, a committee head or a program chairman, you can benefit from humor power. Try using it when you talk to, at, or about your club.

He Believed

When he was asked whether he believed in clubs for women, W. C. Fields replied, "Of course I do. But only after all other means of persuasion have failed."

If you would like to be more persuasive in social-club situations, you can prepare yourself by collecting one-liners and vignettes keyed to your club and its needs.

Membership: "A nudist club advertised only fifty per cent off for new members." Or: "Last month, we had a successful membership drive—very successful. We drove out fifteen members."

Needlecrafts: "Is Mrs. Stewart an active member?"

"Oh, no. She never says a word. She just sits there and embroiders."

Jogging: "I gain weight when I'm running—because I run into every fast-food place I see."

Or: "Whatever happened to your jogging club?"

"We gave it up. It was getting too hard to get lifts from passing cars."

Gardening: "It was a sad occasion. Sadder than a garden-club meeting the day after an early frost." Or: "Make a better lawn and garden, and the world will beat a path across it to your door."

Socially, humor power can help you win!

USE YOUR HUMOR POWER —DON'T ABUSE It

One quip can charge a conversation with lightness and power, but a steady stream of one-liners, aphorisms, and vignettes makes it impossible to *have* a conversation. We've all met the individual who drives us up the wall—in an effort to escape his overpowering humor.

Suppose you're trying to discuss a problem. It could be as simple as picnic plans for a social group. Here's the dialogue:

YOU: It's time we solved this problem.

HE, the "humorist":   Sure. For every problem, there's a simple answer—and it's wrong.

YOU: About the food. Will your wife—

HE: She'd better. I work overtime to buy her labor-saving kitchen aids. Of course, she's on a diet right now. Her doctor told her to eat coconuts and bananas. She hasn't lost weight, but you ought to see her climb trees.

HE (again, and again):   Most people go in for dieting with the wrong equipment. Knives and forks. And there's another thing. Gotta keep in mind that what's on the table soon becomes what's on the chair.

YOU: What does dieting have to do with it? We need a good picnic spot. I thought—

HE: I know just the place. We went there last weekend. Plenty of space. Lots of fresh, pure air—made the kids sick.

YOU: (Speechless!)

HE (guffaws gustily):   Say, you forgot the drinks. Have you tried that new brand, Bullfrog Gin? Drink a little, hop a little, and croak! Oh, did I tell you the one about the drunk who was lying in the gutter? He kept muttering, "I'll get over this wall if it takes me all week."

YOU: (Still speechless!)

HE: Hey, you better stand up. My jokes are going over your head.

YOU: But the problem is—

HE: Two things will solve the world's problems. Religion and booze. Not separately. You gotta drink religiously.

YOU (to yourself): I can't insult him—no way! At least I know he has only one fault. He's unbearable.

Exaggerated? So is some people's use of humor. The same people are the first to laugh at their own jokes—even before they make them.

Humor power is important, but it isn't all of life. Apply it as and when you please. How can you pick the right moment? It helps to remember why you need humor power in personal life. And some reasons why are to give and gain a better picture of yourself, help others develop a stronger self-image, modify your own self-focused moods, and help others modify and improve their moods.

You can transform "why" into "how" when you see others as individuals, not stereotypes. That's vitally important in your personal life. But it may be even more important in your marriage and family life. Read on!

5 Humor Power
in Your Marriage
and Family Life

HE: My wife never will understand money. She thinks a bargain is anything that's fifty per cent off.

SHE: That's why I married *you,* half-wit.

The way some people look for faults, you'd think there was a reward! But that's one form of our traditional he/she humor. Jokes about marriage often stereotype images of dull husband, dumb wife, wife as ruler but drudge, husband as slave but superior being. And he/she humor sometimes plunges to the depths of the wisecrack.

WIFE (bending over husband's hospital bed): You simply can't die, Tom. I don't have a single black dress in my whole wardrobe.

Or HUSBAND (to swimming instructor): Can you teach my wife to drown?

He/she humor reaches toward humor *power* with the hyperbole of stories that contrast the unpleasant—and unlikely— with a hidden point-maker about relationships.

CURIOUS NEIGHBOR: I heard there was some trouble at your house.

WOMAN: Nonsense. My husband and I had words, and I shot him. But that's as far as it went.

While this story certainly exaggerates to the point of unbelievability, it's more than a funny joke. If we examine the sentences "My husband and I had words, and I shot him. But that's as far as it went" we can find the hidden point-maker: It's better to take some words lightly and avoid a serious disagreement.

He/she humor equals humor *power,* with the kind of kidding that prevents bitterness by enabling us to laugh at ourselves.

A husband was asked if he believed in life after death.

"Shucks," said his wife, "he doesn't even believe in life after dinner."

Another husband explained, "My wife and I disagreed. She wanted a new fur coat. I wanted a new car. We compromised. Bought a fur coat and kept it in the garage."

Stereotyped humor claims the typical family consists of a man who makes money and a wife and kids who make that necessary.

"A family man is one who has replaced the money in his wallet with a picture of his wife and kids."

Alert: This same approach has value when we use it to reveal ourselves to others. Through self-directed laughter, we can suggest ways to improve relationships. Some professional performers make a career of laughing at themselves in marriage and family life—notably, Rodney Dangerfield, of "I Don't Get No Respect" fame. He sets himself up as the laughable target of his family.

"I asked my wife to run away with me," quipped Dangerfield. "She said, 'You go.'"

"My son goes to a private school," Dangerfield confided. "I've been trying for two years to get him to tell me where it is."

The closer marriage approaches, it seems, the more biting he/she humor can become. For example: "Husband-hunting is a sport where the animal that gets caught pays for the license."

Humor about dating or courtship (yes, it does still happen!) tends to be tender when we use the think-funny forces of humor *power*.

Even when it's a case of Jeff saying that his beautiful girl friend spoiled their relationship by using four-letter words. Like "don't" and "can't" and "won't."

Or Dad greeting Nancy's beau, "You look different than I expected, Johnny. I thought you had a phone cord growing out of your ear!"

Why should dating or courting couples have all the fun of humor power? Let's consider how we can . . .

KEEP THE LOVE
IN MARRIAGE

"You always hurt the one you love," said the porcupine.

Perhaps we turn put-down humor on our marriage and family life because we deeply love those who are closest to us and feel that they will understand our lapse when we say an uncaring thing. In fact, we *can* laugh more freely with our dearest and closest. But an obligation goes with this truth—to use not bitter, sarcastic humor but happy, dynamic humor *power*.

We owe it to ourselves not to relax into rudeness with our mates and children. Just as we do in other areas of our personal life, we can use our humor power to heal, not hurt.

Before and After

"Keep your eyes wide open before marriage," suggested Ben Franklin, "half shut afterwards."

—Poor Richard's Almanac, 1738

Certainly, humor power from some traditional he/she stories and quips can guide us to understanding. We can learn by laughing at ourselves, for instance in the role of "henpecked husband":

"Tell me, Jim, who's the boss at your house?"

"Jenny bosses the children, the dog, and the parakeet," Jim confessed, "but I lay down the law to the goldfish."

Or in the role of "bossy wife":

"You say your husband's an efficiency expert. Just what does he do?"

"It's hard to explain. But if I did it, he'd call it nagging."

A deeper understanding awaits those who use their humor power in marriage and family life more openly, more effectively, more creatively. Remember that marriage, like humor power, grows stronger through the balance of opposites.

Marriage Makes Scissors

Marriage resembles a pair of shears, so joined that they cannot be separated; often moving in opposite directions, yet always punishing anyone who comes between them.

—SYDNEY SMITH

Chances are, you chose your mate because the two of you can communicate. You admire your mate's humor power when he or she says, "If you really loved me, you would have married somebody else!" (And you may even learn to understand and laugh with the humor power of your kids.) Keep a good thing going, and think funny together.

"We were perfectly happy for twenty-five years."

"Then what happened?"

"We met!"

Laugh with, not at, your spouse and children.

"Every time I complain about the low marks on my daughter's report card, she reminds me she's an exemption on my income tax."

"My wife doesn't care what my secretary looks like, as long as he's efficient."

"My husband's an optimist. He never expects the worst, but when it happens, he makes the most out of it."

Help your family laugh by doing and saying amusing things, just as you would amuse friends or associates on the job.

"One big advantage of bubble gum is, you kids can't ask questions while you're chewing it."

"Sometimes it is better to have loved and lost, than to have to do homework for eight kids."

"I tried to get the color of paint you wanted. But they told me at the paint store that husbands ordering specially mixed colors need signed notes from their wives."

"My garage sale was almost over, and I was really discouraged. A lot of the stuff hadn't sold. So I put up a sign, 'Shoplifting Encouraged.' "

Laugh AT yourself in your marriage and family life. Let everyone know you're human—and humor-powered.

"I quit drinking. Did it for the wife and kidneys."

Dialogue: "My wife drives me to drink."

"You're lucky. Mine makes me walk."

"They make me take the family picture, every time. That way, I'm never in it."

"I always win family arguments. If I lose the first time, I ask for an instant replay."

"My wife has the most wonderful way of winning arguments. Last night, I told her I was going out to play poker, and she said, 'Over my nude body.' "

"My wife has an unusual medical problem. Her arms are getting shorter. I know they're getting shorter—because when we first married, she could reach around me."

"I reminded my husband that when he married me, he promised me the moon. He said, 'And you know why? Because there aren't any stores up there.' "

"My son asked me, 'Daddy, where are the Alps?' Absent-mindedly, I said, 'Ask your mother. She puts everything away.' "

Keeping Her Happy

Only two things are necessary to keep one's wife happy.
The first is to let her think she's having her own way.
The second is to let her have it.

—LYNDON B. JOHNSON

Share and Grow—with Humor Power

"Love makes the world go round, but it's laughter that keeps
us from getting dizzy." Shared humor power can lead the way
to a balance of love and laughter.

Some older persons, I believe, can learn about this from
today's young couples who know how to share their interests.
Of course, that isn't entirely a new idea.

One young man told me, "My father always helped my
mother with the cooking. In fact, he helped himself to the
lion's share of it."

It may have been that young man's wife who said, "My
mother and father shared a serene faith. Both showed it, in the
way they drove the car."

Consider this humorous story, of the put-down variety.

An oldster, in his nineties, said he hoped he and his wife,
who was exactly his age, would share more years of life together.

"I want to live to be a hundred and twenty," he explained,
"and I want my wife to live to a hundred and nineteen."

"Why the difference in years?"

"Because," he said, "I want one year to live in peace."

Contrast that with a real-life anecdote about Patricia and
Mark Mueller of Freehold, New Jersey.

During the first year of their married life, Patricia and
Mark attended the University of Missouri at Rolla. They were
famous on the campus for their shared interest in computer
technology. Famous, too, for a shared physical trait. Red hair.

A caller, phoning to locate Pat and Mark, but not knowing their names, exclaimed, *"You* know—the red-headed computer team!"

As a team, Patricia and Mark thought funny about the incident and shared its humor power with others. No need here for the stereotypes of put-down humor!

At times, though, sharing interests can go too far.

Take the wife who wasn't hooked on fishing trips and didn't want to be found on a hunting trip. Football games weren't her goal, and baseball home runs made her think of running home.

Yet her husband insisted that she go along while he enjoyed those four pastimes.

At last, she begged, "Why can't you be like other husbands and never take me anywhere?"

Alert: With humor power, this wife made an important point: There's a difference between sharing interests and insisting on too much togetherness. As a modern proverb reminds us, "Love means keeping close enough to touch but leaving space enough to grow."

When it's a question of sharing romance, some oldsters know how to laugh at themselves. Witness the elderly man who absolutely refused to marry a charming young woman who fell in love with him.

"My dear, I can't," he told her, gently. "Father and Mother are against it."

"What! At your age, your parents are still living?"

"No, no," he corrected. "I mean Father Time and Mother Nature."

In the sharing of humor power, participation pays. Don't just sit there and laugh with the humor power of your spouse and children. Participate!

Let me illustrate that point with a legendary letter from a woman with ten kids. She listened to a papal encyclical on birth control, then wrote:

"Dear Mr. Pope, If you don't play the game, don't make the rules."

Share, and participate, in humor power. The results can reward with sustaining trust. Here's one view:

Relativity Speaking

Mrs. Albert Einstein was asked, "Do you understand your husband's theory of relativity?"

She shook her head. "But I know my husband, and I know he can be trusted."

Heehaws or Heartwarmers?

In some memorable moments of marriage and family life, the humor of the put-down can scar or destroy. Even laughter may be out of place. Instead of a lusty heehaw, try humor *power* that goes to the heart of the moment. Sometimes, this power hums along so very gently that we may not think of it as humorous. Yet it's rich in merry feeling.

Halina Rodzinski, in her book *Our Two Lives,* tells this story:

At home after the birth of the Rodzinskis' first child, she rested in an upstairs bedroom. Music, full and triumphant, swelled upward. Appropriate—since her husband, Artur, was then director of the New York Philharmonic.

She asked him, "Where did you get the wonderful new radio?"

Rodzinski coaxed her downstairs to a roomful of beaming musicians playing the "Siegfried Idyll"—composed by Richard Wagner in celebration of his son's birth.

Heartwarming!

My most brilliant achievement was my ability to be able to persuade my wife to marry me.

—WINSTON CHURCHILL

To illustrate heartwarming humor power in family life, President Harry S. Truman favored this anecdote:

Shortly after he became President, a visitor called on his mother. "How proud you must be of your boy Harry!" the visitor bubbled.

"Yes, I am," agreed Mrs. Truman, "and I'm just as proud of another fine son. He's out there now, plowing the fields."

Beginning with the wedding, marriage and memorable moments go together. Predictably, Groucho Marx made his first wedding ceremony memorable with insults.

When he married Ruth Johnson, he kidded the minister, "Why are you going so fast? This is a five-buck ceremony. Aren't we entitled to at least five minutes of your time?"

Some twenty years later, he and Ruth were divorced. As they parted, he shook hands with her, saying, "It's been nice knowing you. If you're ever in the neighborhood again, drop in!"

You and I may not have Groucho's way with the insight-producing insult. And we may not have the special advantages that bless some husbands and wives.

One Slight Edge

When the Duke of Windsor, formerly Edward VIII, talked with a group of men about how to make their wives happy, he admitted, "I do have one slight edge over the rest of you.

"It helps in a pinch to remind your bride that you gave up a throne for her."

We do have the opportunity to gain the power of humor and use it in our closest relationships.

Alert: Humor power in your marriage and family life, however, is *not* a handle-with-too-much-care force. Some moments call for the gentle touch, but others demand robust, dynamic humor power, sturdy enough to withstand and reduce the tensions of daily life.

Show Yourself—and See Yourself

After all, who is better prepared to point out your faults than your spouse? When your ego overexpands, who will apply a little deflation? Your kids, of course! We can depend on the humor power that flows from our mates and children to reveal, understand, and improve ourselves. And we can look to the youngsters to help us see ourselves with humor power. Here's another personal example.

When I ask children, "What's your dad like?" they don't often respond, "He loves my mother," or "He's a spiritual man." In fact, they're more likely to say, "He loves cars," or "He works for the XYZ Company."

But sometimes I get this answer: "My dad is a fun guy." With these words, a youngster implies, "My dad isn't pompous. He doesn't take himself too seriously, he thinks funny, and he gives me some free space."

Thinking funny and taking one's self lightly relate, of course, to the fundamentals of humor power. And a parent who, by being "fun," can give a child some "free space" achieves an important goal—because children belong to themselves. In fact, "My dad is a fun guy" can be another way of saying "He loves my mother" and "He's a spiritual man." I would like to have my children say this about me.

Humor-powered wisdom from the young makes the point, even when it's unplanned. That was the case with a Father's Day composition written by an eight-year-old boy: "My father can climb the highest mountain, swim the biggest ocean, fly the fastest plane, and fight the strongest tiger. But most of the time, he just takes out the garbage."

The message also comes through in a story about a father who always took the family driving on Sunday afternoons. One Sunday, he was sick. Mother did the driving, while Dad stayed home. Perhaps he hoped he would be missed, or he may have prided himself on his mastery of the road.

When Mom and the kids returned, Dad asked, "How did you enjoy the drive?"

"It was wonderful, Daddy!" the littlest girl exclaimed. "We didn't see a single bastard."

Humor power can drive points home effectively:

Wife (to husband): "Can't you say we've been married almost twenty-five years, instead of nearly a quarter of a century?"

"I claimed fifty per cent depreciation on myself," a husband said at income-tax time. "My wife says I'm only half the man I used to be."

"You should be glad I don't talk like our new neighbor," said a wife to her husband. "I asked her if she could take a joke, and she answered, 'Sure. I married one.'"

Then there's the wife who told her husband, "I just read a survey proving you're sexier than average."

"Where was this survey taken?" he wanted to know.

Pithily, she replied, "Forest Lawn Cemetery."

And the husband who stared when his wife came into the living room, her hair a mass of rollers: "My gosh, what happened to you?"

"I just set my hair."

He looked at his watch. "What time will it go off?"

Still another husband and wife—call them Mary and John —ordered tulip bulbs for fall planting. Repeatedly, Mary reminded John to plant the bulbs, but he put off the job. Finally, she did it herself.

He was delighted—until spring. The tulips came up, flowered, and in a pattern of glowing colors spelled, "JOHN IS LAZY."

When you open up with humor power, you can create the opportunity to give and gain. And a new perspective may transform put-down stories or quips into helpful suggestions for improving family relationships.

Imagine a husband who arrived home, breathless but triumphant.

"I ran all the way here behind a bus," he panted, "and I saved fifty cents."

Commented his wife, "Why didn't you run behind a taxi and save five dollars?"

Although the story springs from imagination, it can carry a valid message. For instance, you might tell it to your spouse, as a way of saying, "Let's laugh together"—about anything from a financial problem to a tendency toward exaggeration.

Favorite stories of famous personages can give us a fresh point of view. This one illustrates the difference between "laughing at" and "laughing with."

Ike Liked Humor Power

President Eisenhower liked this story, about a friend who was invited to join a golf foursome.

"Sorry," the man said. "My wife doesn't want me to play golf."

"Why worry about her?" another golfer scoffed. "Are you a man or a mouse?"

"I'm a man," the friend answered. "My wife is afraid of mice."

Most probably, Eisenhower's friend pretended to blame his spouse because he didn't want to play golf. More importantly, he was laughing with, not at, his wife. And the gentle message behind his quip was, "She and I share the power to laugh together."

In heated moments or tense situations, an apparent put-down can become an effective reminder. Here's an example:

Another mythical couple quarreled bitterly, until the husband felt ashamed. He called his wife to the window to see an unusual sight—two horses pulling a load of hay up the hill.

"Why can't we pull together like that, up the hill of life?"

"We can't pull together like two horses," the wife replied, "because one of us is a jackass."

Her quip may seem bitter and sharp, but the emotional climate can alter its meaning. After an argument, the wife's quip might be a way of telling her husband, "Yes, I agree with you. Let's laugh together instead of quarreling."

Or she might use the quip in a spirit of fun and play, not in a serious manner. And she and her spouse will be reminded that the half-sting, half-embrace of humor power can heal, not hurt. In any situation, much of humor power depends not on what we say but on what we feel when we say it.

All of us know couples who can't seem to move in harness. Sometimes, we might explain this by saying that:

> When they were married, they were mispronounced man and wife.
>
> —JACKIE GLEASON

> Many a man in love with a dimple makes the mistake of marrying the whole girl.
>
> —STEPHEN LEACOCK

Often, it seems, couples who continually disagree don't know how to share humor power, or how to use it to solve problems and make helpful points about each other's behavior.

"My wife/husband doesn't have a sense of humor," one or the other will say. Then, he/she proves personal possession of sarcasm.

"My wife is as sharp as a pin. She's pointed in one direction and headed in another."

"My husband is so stupid, he tried to knock on a revolving door. When he took an IQ test, he couldn't even spell IQ."

From one perspective, those examples show harsh humor. Husband and wife are laughing at, not with, each other. But a closer examination reveals the more serious problem of low self-esteem. They're anxious and insecure about their own intelligence. No wonder they can't relate to each other! Often "My wife/husband is stupid" equals "I think I'm stupid."

Fortunately, all of us also know couples who have found

the secret of kidding each other, thinking funny, and laughing together. We take pleasure in their company, and we want to spend more time with them. What's more, we want to be like them, in our marriage and family life.

We are—when we show ourselves and see ourselves with humor power. An example from public life reminds us.

Be Constructive!

Will Rogers knew the value of using humor to heal, not hurt. He declared, "My epitaph is going to read, 'I joked about every prominent man of my time, but I never met a man I didn't like.'"

As you joke about—or better, with—the prominent man or woman in your private life . . .

Enjoy the Differences

"My wife and I have our differences. But, like a Californian after an earthquake, we always say, 'With all your faults, I love you still.'"

When you and your spouse have differences, laugh together—about the differences. Especially the vital difference!

After lecturing on his subject, men and women, Dr. Alfred Kinsey invited questions.

"Dr. Kinsey, I've listened to you with great interest," a woman said, "but I still think men and women are pretty much the same. In your opinion, what is the vital difference?"

"Madam," he responded, "I cannot conceive."

No Smoking

I kissed my first woman and smoked my first cigarette on the same day. Since then, I've never had time for tobacco.

—ARTURO TOSCANINI

Humor power sheds light on the differences, and on the changing scene.

"Your whole life turns around when you hit middle age. You start to eat, and you feel sexy. You go to bed, and you feel hungry."

"By the time a man is able to read a woman like a book, his eyes go bad."

W. C. Fields said, regretfully, "It was a woman who started me on the road to drink—and I never wrote to thank her." He also remarked, "There may be some things better than sex, and some things may be worse. But there is nothing exactly like it."

"He takes vitamin E; she takes iron pills. When he's ready, she's rusty."

"You can't blame a wife for being pooped after twelve hours of housework. Face it. If you had to list the ten greatest aphrodisiacs of all time, Draino wouldn't be one of them."

"A loser heard his wife was sleeping with his best friend. So he went home and shot his dog."

With humor power, we recognize and relate to the changing scene.

My wife went off to Tulsa for a few days, and I was a bachelor again. Back yonder twenty years or so ago, when she went away, she would tell me, "Stay at home and behave yourself." Now she says, "Don't forget to water my plants and don't go to sleep with the TV on."

A married friend planned a bachelor trip to the Thousand Islands. He wasn't too happy about his wife's reaction.

"She didn't say I couldn't go. She told me to spend a week on each one."

When I asked a young chap about his marriage plans, he told me, "I'm going to stay single till I meet a woman like the one Grandpa married."

"They don't make women like that any more," I warned.

"Sure they do," he said. "Grandpa married her just yesterday. He met her in a disco."

A husband and wife went to a convention in Miami Beach. When they tried to check into their hotel, they found the place packed—and with no record of their reservation.

The desk clerk soothed the irate husband. "We'll put you in the bridal suite."

"Ridiculous!" the husband exploded. "We've been married for fifteen years."

"So?" commented the clerk. "If I put you in the ballroom, you wouldn't have to dance, would you?"

Familiar Scene

Familiarity breeds contempt, and children.

—MARK TWAIN

Some commentators on the changing scene tell us that new roles in marriage and family life are going to make a big difference. All this sexual equality can change the way we embrace others with humor power!

Traditionally, we joke about theories that women:

Spend too much, and are always late. "The only thing my wife does on time is buy."

Won't admit their age. "My wife says she's approaching her twenty-eighth birthday, but she faces in the wrong direction."

Can't keep secrets. "There's no truth in that. Women *can* keep a secret. It just takes more of them to do it."

And that men are:

Thoughtless and inconsiderate. "You're so wrapped up in golf," a wife accused, "you don't even remember our wedding day."

"Sure I do," her husband protested. "That was the day I sank that thirty-five-foot putt."

Unobservant and unappreciative. "My husband hasn't taken a good look at me in five years," another wife complained. "If anything happened to me, I'm afraid he wouldn't be able to identify the body."

Bad-tempered and critical. "When a wife said, playfully, 'You need a self-starter to get you up in the morning,' her husband answered, grouchily, 'No I don't. Not with a crank like you around.'"

Changing roles could inspire us to power our humor with a fresh approach. After all, sex is something we are, not something we do.

We men may not see ourselves in the role of the father who paced the floor with a crying baby while Mother relaxed in bed.

Muttered Dad, "Nobody ever asked *me* how I manage to combine marriage and a career."

But we can't shrug off the new-roles topic with a quip, such as, "I know a woman who's pregnant, and she isn't sure it's hers." Or: "The liberated woman of today doesn't chase a man. Just like a mousetrap doesn't chase a mouse." Almost certainly, those one-liners will be perceived as laughing at others. And we won't gain, but we may create antagonism and resentment.

Still, our humor power will cause us to consider this question: "If God was satisfied with Adam, how come He made Eve so different?"

Humorist Joey Adams claimed women's liberation has gone too far. "I'm writing a book about men's liberation," he declared. "It will be published—just as soon as my wife okays it."

At the library, a man held the door open as a woman approached.

"If you're holding that door for me because I'm a lady, forget it," she said.

"No, madam," he replied. "I'm holding the door out of respect for your age."

Male chivalry isn't dead, though. Just the other day in South Bend, I saw a woman drop a package on the sidewalk. A man kicked it back to her.

Herbert Mines observed changing roles from his perspective as president of an executive search firm. Spotting a trend at the executive level, Mines believes many more women will want to combine home and economic life in the next decade, with more sharing of roles by husband and wife.

"Marriages are going to be more exciting, relationships are

going to be more satisfying," he predicts, "and it's going to be more fun for both parties."

With that happy prospect, who would want to stay single? Some will—and they'll need humor power!

It's tough to be a bachelor. My wife says you can always recognize one when he comes into the supermarket and asks, "Where's the toast?"

A bachelor friend complained to me, "I'm getting old."

Of course, I told him he looked as young as ever.

"No, I don't," he insisted. "People used to ask me, 'Why don't you marry?' Now they ask, 'Why didn't you marry?'"

A hills woman came up with an answer for that question. Setting out on a trip, she approached the ticket counter at the bus station.

The ticket seller, bored and weary, asked, "Single?"

"Ain't none of your business," the hills woman said, "but I could of married a dozen times, if I wanted to support a worthless SOB like you."

TAKE THE COMEDY
OUT OF LOVE

Humor power can support us through many difficulties of marriage and family life. But what about problems so serious that separation or divorce looms? Such problems might be prevented by taking the comedy out of love, through a humor-powered perspective. Let me develop that thought in terms of a mythical couple, the Traders.

The Traders aren't interested in giving and gaining; they're interested in receiving without sharing. A Trader almost never asks himself or herself, "Do I try to do things that please him or please her? Do I go out of my way? Do I find myself offering sacrifices in effort and time without expecting some kind of reciprocal act?"

Instead, a Trader is more likely to complain, "I waited ten minutes for you today. Well, you're going to wait twenty minutes for me tomorrow." Or: "I'll do this if you'll do that." And, when problems develop, each Trader blames the other.

The Traders may talk about love, but what they're talking about is a trade, not a gift. Theirs is the comedy—and tragedy —of love.

In fact, "The Comedy of Love" is the title of one of my presentations. And I'm often asked, "What do you mean, Herb? What's the comedy of love?" The way I answer this is: "It's comical that we spend so much time, effort, and money trying to make ourselves lovable. But it's tragic how little we do to make ourselves loving." As psychologist Erich Fromm wrote, most people think in terms of being loved, instead of their capacity to love.

So the real question to ask ourselves may be, "Are you and I so busy getting make-up and clothes to be lovable that we don't try to learn how to be loving?" We can see the idea of becoming lovable reflected in the names of men's colognes: Top Brass, Brut, Trouble, Cow Pasture, or you name them! And what about women's colognes? My Sin, Tabu, Evening in Paris, Morning at the Holiday Inn—again, you name them, they've got them.

It helps to be lighthearted, but there's more tragedy than comedy in the efforts we make to be lovable. You'll recognize the comedy/tragedy in some familiar remarks—by the husband who says:

"I married her because she was such a beauty. Now she thinks only of her looks."

Or: "I married her because she was frail and petite. Now I want to get rid of her because she's weak and helpless."

Familiar, too, is the wife who says:

"I married him because I thought he'd provide a good living. Now all he does is think about business."

Or: "I married him because he was so steady and sensible. Now I want to get rid of him because he's dull and boring."

And then there are the husband and wife who say:

"We married because of this tremendous sexual attraction. Now we don't have anything in common."

Marriages based on infatuation or mutual attraction depend almost entirely on physical traits, personal pleasure, and shared curiosity. They are almost devoid of concern, understanding, and insight.

Forget about calling this love, call it some sort of trade! Here's another example of the Traders' comedy/tragedy:

SHE: If it weren't for my money, you wouldn't have those fancy clothes, that fancy ring, that beautiful watch, and that car.

HE: Yes, and if it weren't for your money, you wouldn't have me.

Let's sum it up: Give, don't trade.

Love is an attitude between those who share many things in common—interests, points of view, errors, even failures. And they share these things to the degree that they are stronger together than each one is alone.

How does humor power apply to this kind of sharing? Shared laughter, I believe, can increase our opportunity to prevent big failures.

And now, let me share some serious suggestions.

To help love last . . .

* Avoid being angry at the same time.
* Speak loudly to each other—only when the house is on fire.
* Avoid taunting your mate with a past mistake.
* Never part for a day without loving words to remember.
* Never let the sun go down on anger or grievance.
* Never forget the happy hours of early love.

Oil Relationships—Ease Strain

Set the balance wheel of marriage and family life moving more smoothly. Ease tensions and strain. Oil the wheel with humor power! This power can be effective in helping us admit it when we're wrong—as we may occasionally be.

You had an argument with your wife or husband. Suddenly, you realize the argument began because of your behavior. Admit it—by poking fun at yourself. Follow the example of the husband who told this story.

FRIEND: How did you come out in the argument with your wife?

HUSBAND: Oh, she came crawling to me on her hands and knees.

FRIEND: That so?

HUSBAND: Yes. She said, "Come out from under that bed, you coward."

You were not as generous as you meant to be with a special-occasion gift. Admit it, humor-powerfully.

"I gave my wife a three-piece sweater set for her birthday. A ball of yarn—and two knitting needles."

"At Christmas, my daughter said she wanted an encyclopedia for school. I said, 'Nothing doing. You can walk to school, just like I did.'"

You forgot the special occasion. Admit it, and let humor power help.

It might help your wife to think funny about your forgetfulness if you say, as you present a belated gift, "I asked at the jewelers, 'What's a good gift for a birthday last week?'"

And, if you're the wife in this situation, your humor-powered response might be, "I know you're a man of rare gifts. You always forget birthdays and anniversaries."

At times, an outsider's humor power can reveal our mistaken behavior.

After a husband had veered between this gift and that gift for about thirty minutes, he asked the saleswoman, "If you were my wife, what would you want for our anniversary?"

Said she, "A divorce!"

One grouch told me his wife kept hinting about something for her neck. So he gave her a cake of soap.

Advice columns in the newspapers offer some interesting hints.

One letter asked, "What's the worst thing a wife can get on her twenty-fifth wedding anniversary?"

Answer: "Morning sickness!"

You're a wife, and you complain that you've had it, with housework, a passel of feisty kids, a TV set always tuned to the football game. But you know complaints will get you nowhere. Admit it!

Last Gasp

Grumbling is the death of love.

—Marlene Dietrich

Make your points with humor power.

"I understand now why women get divorces because of the eternal triangle. They're tired of making breakfast, lunch, and dinner."

"It's sad. We have a six-year-old, and the only four-letter word he doesn't know is soap."

"I told my daughter about sex. It leads to housework!"

"At least our son's report card shows he isn't taking any mind-expanding drugs."

"I'm joining a new organization called 'Wives Anonymous.' When you phone them, they send someone over to talk your husband out of watching football on Sunday afternoon."

Your kids delight you—and mystify you. You don't always understand them. Admit it, and bridge the gap with your humor power.

"The more I see of today's young adults, the more I'm convinced I was never their age."

"No wonder it's tough to communicate with our kids. Half the things happening today are unheard of. The other half are unspeakable!"

"It's hard to understand some youngsters. Kids who refuse to eat spinach grow up and stand in line to buy yogurt."

"I spent a small fortune on my kids' education, and another small fortune on their teeth. The only difference is, they still use their teeth."

"Greg has an almost limitless supply of energy. That's because he conserves it so well."

"I figure Mary has a brilliant future. She just wrote to tell us she won't be living at home this summer, so we can rent out her room. And send the money to her."

" 'I'm old enough to live my own life and have my own apartment,' our teen-age daughter told us. 'Now, all I need is a bigger allowance.' "

Mother and son were talking about his girl friend.

"What does she like about you?" Mother asked.

"That's easy," said the son, modestly. "She thinks I'm handsome, fun, smart, talented, and a good dancer."

"And what do you like about her?"

"That she thinks I'm handsome, fun, smart . . ."

Your kids have a winning way with humor power—more winning maybe than yours. Admit it! Listen, and learn from them how to be more effective.

Children seem to learn early how to communicate and motivate through humor power. For example, they may ask for something they don't want or expect in order to get what they need—as the following dialogue illustrates.

BOY: Mom says I can't have a dog.

FRIEND: You're not going at it the right way. Don't ask for a dog. Ask for a baby brother. Then you'll get a dog!

In addition, we gain humor power from our youngsters' fresh perspective. For example:

A father scolded his noisy daughter. "Didn't you promise you'd be quiet? And didn't I promise you a spanking if you weren't?"

"Yes, Daddy," daughter agreed, "but I broke my promise, so it's okay if you don't keep yours."

And we learn how to take ourselves lightly when youngsters help us open up and see our shortcomings.

Father and son spent a weekend camping out in the woods.

"There now, wasn't that fun?" Dad asked.

"I guess so," said the son. "Only next time, could we bring Mother and the catsup?"

Intentionally or not, our kids discover how to focus their humor power on our interests—and win.

Consider the child of a performer whose contract was up for renewal in the forthcoming TV season. Rushing home on the last day of school, the youngster exclaimed, "Daddy, Daddy, here's my report card."

"Did you pass?"

"Oh, I did better than that," the child said, confidently. "I got held over for another term."

Sometimes, young humor power sees the point before we do.

Another father was showing his little daughter his and her mother's wedding album.

Puzzled, the child looked at the photographs. Suddenly, her face brightened. "I see!" she said. "That was when you got Mommy to come and work for us."

Young adults in the family see and show their parents' roles with humor power.

One daughter borrowed the family car for a date. Later, her boy friend asked, "What did your father say about our car accident?"

"Do you want me to leave out the bad words?"

"Yes."

"He didn't say anything."

Asked which books other than the Bible had helped most, a student answered, "My mother's cookbook and my father's checkbook."

Then there's the young fellow whose surgeon father specialized in spinal surgery. He called Dad "a disc jockey."

Parents can return the compliment of humor power. For example:

"My son had to give up his career because of fallen arches," a woman told her neighbor.

"He was an athlete?"

"No," said Mom, "an architect."

Look Fast

Reminiscing about his childhood, Sam Levenson recalled a visit to a museum. A string of little Levensons moved too slowly to please their father, who said, "Look, kids, if you have to stop and look at everything, you're not going to see anything."

We know they're growing up when they're more worried about us embarrassing them than we are about their embarrassing us! As our children grow from seeing us as all-wise and all-wonderful to seeing us with humor power, we're right to be encouraged. It's proof we are communicating by letting them see *our* humor power.

Play Down Pride

We, of course, think our kids are the brightest, most talented, most likely to succeed of any youngsters ever born. Our neighbors, friends, and associates are more apt to be patient with that perspective if we, tactfully, play down our pride, through humor power.

A father boasted to a friend, "My daughter's piano lessons are already paying off."

When the friend looked doubtful, Dad followed up with, "After listening to her practice, my neighbor offered to sell me his house for one third the market price."

Leave it to a proud grandmother to announce, "My grandson is smarter than Abe Lincoln. Already, he can say the

Gettysburg Address, and he's only eight years old. Lincoln didn't say it until he was fifty."

Grandmothers may feel the need for satirical humor power. That was the case with a woman whose four grandchildren spent a month with her.

She told friends, "Their visit made me doubly happy."

"How was that?"

"I was happy when they came, and I was happy when they left."

Grandmothers and grandfathers, sisters and brothers, sisters-in-law and brothers-in-law, aunts and uncles and cousins by the dozens—or ourselves in any of these roles—all are part of a richer, broader family life, offering us the opportunity to laugh and think funny together.

And we may even learn to laugh with one member of the family who is too often regarded as a stereotype—mother-in-law. We might see her as grandmother.

A St. Paul woman reinforced that point effectively with her individual humor power. When her daughter married and moved to a distant city, she was asked, "Are you going to visit your daughter and new son-in-law?"

"No, I thought I'd wait till they have their first baby," she sparkled. "I've noticed grandmothers are a lot more welcome than mothers-in-law!"

Mothers-in-law, wives, husbands, children, friends, and neighbors can help us give and gain with humor power. And so can our associates on the job! Let's move on, to work.

6 Humor Power on Your Job

Whatever you do for a living, whether you're a beginner or a seasoned pro, boss or employee, company owner or middle manager, humor power can glorify your job. It will help you communicate with and motivate others, solve problems—in particular, people problems—and deal successfully with difficult situations. On the job, we are *not* effective if we're more interested in fixing the blame than we are in fixing the communications breakdown.

Humor power will help you win. This is especially true when what you need is not merely to move all the paper work from the "in" basket to the "out" basket, but to achieve more by innovative action—and, by your example, lead others to do the same.

Humor power will help you in your on-the-job relationships. That's true, and rewardingly so, when you hope to be somebody—somebody who removes obstacles, reflects an optimistic outlook, and wins liking and trust.

How can you fix communications breakdowns, influence and inspire others, and win liking and trust? Three guides to humor power can help: (1) Share laughter with others, to help them understand that you and they have objectives in common; (2) Open up, and admit that you, too, make mistakes;

and (3) Think funny about yourself, and take your honors and rewards lightly. And three examples from top-level executives can be applied to help you.

Share laughter with others; find a common ground.

Even if you and I seem to have conflicting interests, shared laughter reveals the goals we also share.

Frederick R. Kappel, as top executive officer of American Telephone and Telegraph Company, conducted a stockholders' meeting where the emotional climate was especially stormy. Tension mounted as stockholders questioned Kappel, criticized, and complained.

One woman asked persistent questions about AT&T's contributions to charity, which she felt should be increased. "How much did AT&T give to charity last year?" she challenged. And when Kappel quoted figures in the millions of dollars, she quipped, "I think I'm going to faint."

With a straight face, Kappel replied, "That would be helpful."

Then tensions relaxed as most stockholders—including his challenger—laughed. With seemingly hostile humor converted to humor power, Kappel humanized himself, lightened the moment, and gave and gained an awareness of mutual anxieties. And he communicated an important message: "This corporation is aware of humanity's needs. We do care, and we do share your concern."

Open up. Show others it's all right to make and admit mistakes.

At twenty-six, Henry Ford II became president of the Ford Motor Company, while FMC was third in the automotive industry and losing $9 million a month. He succeeded in turning the company around, with innovation, experiment, and, inevitably, some errors.

Asked whether he would do anything different a second time around, he said, "You only learn by your mistakes, so I don't suppose you *can* do it differently. You'd just make different mistakes."

The tuition may be high, but our mistakes do teach us! If

we open up and admit them, we can succeed—as Henry Ford II did.

Think funny about yourself; take your honors and rewards lightly.

When Roger Blough was named chairman of the board at U.S. Steel back in the 1950s, he was asked to comment on his new status. He refused to get excited or to plan a celebration.

"After all," Blough pointed out, "it isn't as if the Pittsburgh Pirates had won a baseball game."

By taking himself lightly, Blough showed he wasn't pompous or puffed up, put his honors in perspective, and made himself memorable. What's more, I'll venture to suggest that he strengthened his self-image.

At this point, you may feel like saying, "Just a minute, Herb. What you're sharing with us sounds great for people who've already reached the top. But I'm just starting out in the working world. How can humor power help me move ahead?"

Let me answer this question with some more examples:

Alice H. was a receptionist for a small business firm. She dealt with in-person callers, phone callers, her associates, and her boss. In her spare time, she did some typing, too. Alice needed humor power, possessed it, and applied it.

Self-important phone callers posed a difficult problem—for example, the man who called and demanded, "I want to speak to your boss."

"May I tell him who's calling?" asked Alice.

"Connect me with your boss," the phone caller insisted. "I want to speak to him right now."

"I'm sorry," Alice said gently. "He pays me to answer the telephone, and it does seem silly. Nine times out of ten, it's for him."

And the phone caller laughed, then gave his name and telephone number. The next step? Alice seems certain to move ahead, for she helped the caller laugh with her, feel better about his temporary failure, and still feel friendly toward her boss.

In fact, Alice carried out the role of a personnel manager by coping with people problems in her receptionist's job.

Whatever our on-the-job role may be, each of us is a personnel manager who needs humor power to help us give and gain a better self-image—and a better job.

While she was going to school, Beth K. worked part-time as a salesclerk in a small store. On her first full-time job, she moved up rapidly from typist to secretary. When she felt she needed a more challenging job, she went to an employment agency.

A consultant at the agency discussed job fields where Beth might find opportunity. "Tell me," the consultant asked, "what's your experience in merchandising?"

"Please tell me what 'merchandising' is," Beth quipped, "and then I'll tell you what my experience is."

Sure enough, after the consultant defined merchandising, Beth came up with a resumé of experience which led to an exciting job. (In case you're wondering, the consultant's definition was, "Planning and promoting sales of a product or service." And Beth's new job was in advertising.)

Why was Beth's quip effective? Although it wasn't the kind of quip that makes everyone burst into laughter, it did apply humor power. Beth kidded herself, admitted she didn't know exactly what merchandising meant, and showed that she took herself lightly and her job goals seriously.

Importantly, Beth's openness helped her gain because it showed her a more complete picture of herself. And she found that her part-time job as a salesclerk had given her more experience in merchandising than she realized. When we can focus our humor power on ourselves and develop a total picture, we will gain!

While giving and gaining with humor power may not lead to instant promotion, it can help us. For example:

Ron G., a clerk in an accounting department, received an empty pay envelope. He didn't stamp his foot and scream. Instead, he asked the payroll department, "What happened? Did my deductions finally catch up with my salary?"

Of course, Ron received his pay. In addition, he showed that he could think funny about errors, instead of taking himself too seriously and complaining about others' goofs. He shared humor power! When we can see the funny side of on-the-job situations, we can win our associates' co-operation—something we need, if we're to move ahead.

Barry K. held a desk job in the shipping department of a large manufacturing firm. When another company took over the firm, Barry stayed afloat in the waves of personnel changes. But his new co-workers seemed unfriendly—until Barry applied humor power.

"They don't dare fire me," he explained. "I'm always too far behind in my work."

By laughing at himself, Barry helped his new associates laugh with him, and helped to develop friendly, co-operative on-the-job relationships. And if Barry's one-liner revealed that he did have a tendency to put off today's work until tomorrow, it also gave him greater self-knowledge. With humor power, he could examine his fault—procrastination—objectively, improve his performance, and gain.

Suppose that humor power has helped you advance toward your job goal. Then, it's time to . . .

Keep Moving Ahead— Managing with Success

On your way to the top, you will encounter obstacles as well as opportunities. And one obstacle—or opportunity—will probably be the difficulty of coping, emotionally, with your new role. As part of its price, success demands that we put aside many of our skills and specialties to concentrate on relating to and motivating people.

This can be difficult to accept, emotionally. If you felt you were the world's best teacher, secretary, accountant, or tightener of bolts, you might not be totally happy, at first, in a new role as principal, supervisor, manager, or foreman. After all, it's more comfortable to use skills than it is to handle a constant flow of people problems.

On the middle-management level, for instance, you will need to modify and improve others' moods, smooth relationships between co-workers, and help your associates untangle their person-to-job-related problems. All of this poses quite a challenge. But it's a challenge humor power can help you handle and enjoy.

And if you have used humor power to help yourself advance, you'll be prepared to think funny about setbacks, to open up with self-focused laughter and you-directed concern for others, and, above all, to take yourself lightly and your new role seriously.

Once more, I can best illustrate this with true-to-life examples of the way humor-powered managers cope with their roles.

Ellis J. headed one department of a large corporation. And one of his emotional problems as a manager was, "Do the people in my department really like me?" Fortunately, Ellis had a sense of humor, which he began to apply as humor power. Observe his humor power at work in this Christmas-season incident:

Ellis returned from a business meeting to find his staff gathered around a desk and humming the "Hallelujah Chorus" from Handel's *Messiah*. His entry was enough to send everyone scurrying back to work. But instead of frowning or grumbling, Ellis said:

"I don't think you have a handle on that."

Again, that wasn't the kind of one-liner which produces belly laughs. But it worked effectively. With a smile, the staff accepted Ellis's gently implied criticism. By laughing with staff members about their humming instead of scolding them for loafing, Ellis found a better way to say, "Stop goofing off!" What's more, Ellis focused a new perspective on his problem: "Do the people in my department really like me?"

"If I like others and can give them what they need by laughing with them," he discovered, "then I will gain what I need—a better relationship with everyone on the staff."

Another achiever, Doris M., needed help from humor

power to see and understand that she was indeed a winner. As public relations co-ordinator for a major company, Doris had the responsibility of improving the company's image in the eyes of the public. Other managers marveled at her ability to cope with the pressures of time, tight deadlines, and constantly changing public attitudes.

But Doris worried about her self-image. During a one-and-a-half-year period, she hired, trained, and then lost three secretaries, who took jobs with other companies. "What's wrong with me?" she wondered. "Why can't I keep a secretary?"

An associate helped her see herself. "All three secretaries moved on to better jobs in public relations," the associate pointed out. "You should be proud you helped them to get ahead."

"The trouble with me is, I'm in the wrong profession," Doris kidded herself. "I should have been a teacher. But I'm too good at teaching. Next time, I won't train my secretary so well."

By laughing at herself, Doris gained a more confident self-image. And she was still able to laugh when her next well-trained secretary moved on to a better job.

If you can apply humor power to help others move up the ladder, too, you will keep moving ahead. And if you need another incentive to develop humor power on your job, you might consider this:

Business Believes in the Power of Humor

All kinds of businesses, large and small, place a high value on humor power. Top-level corporate executives apply humor power to change their image and improve the public's picture of the corporation. Leaders and managers on every level turn to humor power for help in the selection and training of associates.

Let me back up these statements by giving a few statistics

and examples. And, for the purpose of this discussion, let's agree that when the words "humor" and "sense of humor" are used they mean "humor power."

Major executives of 329 leading companies participated in a humor-opinion poll. William Hodge, president of a management consulting firm, conducted the poll and found that:

Ninety-seven per cent of these executives agreed, "Humor is valuable in business."

Sixty per cent believed that a sense of humor helps determine the extent of an individual's business success.

When Alvin Nagelberg, writer of business features for the "Chicago Tribune Service," interviewed some executives who took part in the poll he came up with these top-management opinions:

William O. Beers, chairman of Kraft, Inc., valued a sense of humor in executives. "It's an important indication that [an executive] has an active, flexible mind," Beers said. "These people usually don't take themselves too seriously, and they make better decisions."

Henry C. Goodrich, president of Inland Container Corporation, viewed humor from the perspective of creating a compatible, happy staff. "It's a fundamental principle," he said, "that if you do something you enjoy, you'll be a better employee and a better employer."

Another indicator of the growing interest in humor as a tool of business communication comes from Robert Orben, humorist and creator of a topical humor service. Within the last decade, Bob says, the profile of subscribers to the service has changed dramatically. Business users predominate—instead of the former blend of entertainers, politicians, educators, and others.

What about humor as a yardstick for employee potential? Recently, Michael E. Hurst shared his views on that subject with me. Mike holds a top-level executive post with a Florida firm that operates restaurants. And he rates humor high on the list of employee assets. It's especially important, he says, for the people "out front" who welcome the public.

When interviewing and selecting personnel, Mike counsels, "Look for the sparklers; look for the people with pizazz. They laugh at themselves, and they smile easily."

What's more, he asks prospective employees this key question: "What funny thing ever happened to you?" When the interviewee can't remember a funny happening, it helps if he can make a humorous remark, Mike adds.

As a speaker, I find more and more high-level leaders want to humanize their image in the eyes of their associates and the public. These leaders encourage me to laugh with them. So, I might kid a prominent person by saying:

"Oh, my gosh, look at you! Anybody else hurt in the accident?"

Or, I might ask, "Isn't it awful about the fire at Joe's house? He lost his entire library. Both books. And one of them he hadn't even colored yet."

Laughing with others increases my opportunities to laugh at myself. If I don't seize those opportunities, I could become a loser. And on the lecture platform, a speaker is a loser who knows laughter is the best medicine, but can't get the cap off the bottle.

On your job, humor creates the power to understand, influence, and inspire others—and the power to understand and accept yourself. You can begin to achieve this by . . .

Looking on the Bright Side
—with Humor Power

"What do I like about you? Well, you've never been arrested for embezzlement."

Most of us wouldn't go that far to search out a likable trait in a co-worker or boss. But thinking about negatives can yield positive results. A humor-powered perspective enables us to focus on the bright side of our associates' behavior, instead of on their mistakes. And we give and gain understanding of human errors, plus better working relationships.

Henry Bright, Victorian writer, learned about that from

his heavy-drinking butler. He fired the bibulous butler and, while writing a reference, told him, "I'm saying you're honest and good at your job, but I can't say you're sober."

"Sir," suggested the butler, "couldn't you say, 'Frequently sober'?"

In our own era, a farmer was called on to give a reference for a live-in worker. Affirmed the farmer, "He has a good appetite and has no trouble sleeping."

A lazy clerk fiddled around while his irate boss burned.

"You're the most useless person I ever saw," the boss flared. "You don't do an hour's work a month. Tell me one single way the firm benefits from employing you."

The clerk pondered, then responded, "When I go on vacation, there's no extra work thrown on the others."

Then there was the laborer who, in moving materials at a construction site, was carrying very light loads. The foreman had something to say about that.

In the expurgated version, he said, "What do you think you're doing? Look at the big loads the other men are carrying."

"Well," said the laborer, "I can't help it if they're too lazy to make as many trips as I do."

A boxer came to, head reeling, after a second-round knockout. "I sure did scare that other guy in the first round," he gloated. "He was afraid he was going to kill me."

When you develop the humor power to understand another's perspective, you open the door to better communication on the job.

Listen in as a speaker denounces the evils of drink.

"I wish all beer and liquor were at the bottom of the sea," he cries.

"So do I!" calls a voice from the audience.

"Sir, I congratulate you," declares the speaker. "I can see you're a dedicated man. May I ask, what is your role in life?"

"Sure. I'm a deep-sea diver."

Imagine a robber's wife telling him she needs money. And telling him and telling him.

"All right, don't nag. I'll get you some money. As soon as the bank closes."

Of course, I know you can't identify with the robber's perspective! But laughing with others who hold widely varying jobs can help you develop your own self-image—and focus your empathy toward others. Then, you can . . .

Make Your Points
—and Win

Some people seem to handle their jobs like a mosquito in a nudist camp. They know what to do, but they can't figure out where to start.

If we sting an associate who mishandles a job with a pointed criticism, we set up a losing situation. Our associate loses self-confidence, and we lose trust, without winning cooperation. But "you-directed" understanding of others opens a door to communication.

Win with humor power! Make a suggestion instead of a criticism, and laugh with your associate about the on-the-job problem that led to the mistake. Then, both you and your associate win. What's more, your associate will gain the freedom to laugh with you.

Here's one way to give-and-gain, or win-and-win, in a simple but familiar job situation:

A supervisor said to a staff member, "I need five copies of this progress report, right away." The staff member pressed a button on the copying machine, and presto, twenty-five copies rolled out.

"I don't want twenty-five copies," the supervisor snapped.

And the staff member smiled. "Sorry, but you've got them."

Then they shared a chuckle about an in-common problem —the inhumanity of office machines. With a lighthearted response, the staff member relaxed tension and won appreciation for her emotional balance of seriousness and thinking funny.

Her boss won, too. In a more relaxed mood, he realized

he had overlooked an opportunity to communicate better with other departments. And the twenty extra copies helped other supervisors appreciate what his department was doing.

Humor power works to win-and-win when problems spring from company-to-client relationships, too:

As past-due bills mount higher, they often become an acute problem. In fact, if the client is a regular, substantial purchaser of products or services, the problem is usually handled from the top—by the company president.

"You know, Eddie, we appreciate your business," the president might say to the client at lunch or dinner, "but your account has been overdue for ten months now. Already, we've carried you longer than your mother did."

The problem will probably be solved, thanks to the president's ability to think funny about it. In the business world, humor power can be applied to treat delicate subjects with tenderness.

A winning attitude about tough jobs can help us avoid mistakes and prevent failure. Samuel Siegel, professor of law, illustrated this as he lectured on courtroom procedure.

"When you're fighting a case, if you have the facts on your side, hammer on the facts," Professor Siegel suggested. "If you have the law on your side, hammer on the law."

"If you don't have the facts or the law," a student queried, "then what do you do?"

"In that case, hammer on the table!"

Professor Siegel's answer suggested: When the problems of your profession are really tough, try to approach them by thinking funny.

To make a point about your tough job and its problems, apply humor power. You might tell this story:

En route to Washington to join a protest, an Alabama farmer traveled by plane for the first time. Although he admired the indoor plumbing on the plane, he pointed out, "A sign said, 'Don't Flush Over Cities.' That shows what people think of rural America."

The farmer's humor-powered message was: Look at others' problems from their perspective.

Tough problem? "Think positive," one manager suggested, viewing the daily grind with humor power. "To hell with reality!"

See yourself in one of these situations:

You're the boss, and the pace of business is steady. Steady? It's motionless! Say to the staff, "Do you realize the last time an order came into this office was two weeks ago? And that was for two coffees and a jelly doughnut."

You're a sales manager, and sales have been disappointing. Disappointing? You'd be happier if you had a toothache, just to take your mind off that headache. Motivate your sales force with winning humor power.

"The enemies of every good salesman are loafing, liquor, and living it up. Gentlemen, I have to congratulate you on the way you've learned to love your enemies!"

You're selling—to fussy customers. Fussy? If you were giving away money, they'd insist on engraving their own. Sting them with the half-caress of humor power for a winning result. If they're fussing about price, for example, take a hint from the salesman in an auto showroom when a young couple objected to the price of a compact car.

"That's almost the cost of a big car," the husband complained.

Said the salesman, "If you want economy, you have to pay for it!"

You say these illustrations don't apply to you, because your job isn't selling? Whatever you do for a living, it's bound to involve

HUMOR POWER, SELLING—and You!

The same humor power that makes salesmen great can make you more effective on your job.

Everybody lives by selling something.

—ROBERT LOUIS STEVENSON

People who sell show us how we can win with humor power on the job:

A young woman achieved an amazing record in door-to-door selling of the Encyclopaedia Britannica. How?

"Easily," she twinkled. "I make my calls when both husband and wife are at home. I deliver my sales pitch to the husband—in a very low voice. The wife listens to every word!"

A new traveling salesman talked over his troubles with an old-timer on the road. "I'm not doing too well," he said. "Every place I go, I get insulted."

"Too bad," sympathized the old-timer. "I can't understand it. In more than forty years of traveling the road, I've had my samples tossed out the window, I've been thrown out myself, I've been kicked down the stairs, and I've even been punched in the nose. But I guess I'm lucky. I've never been insulted."

People who sell show us how, with humor power, we can take our jobs more seriously. For example:

When a friend visited his office, a salesman said, "Look at that chair. It cost me five thousand dollars."

"Impossible! That chair isn't worth even five hundred dollars."

"Maybe not, but five thousand is what it cost me. I was sitting in it when I should have been going out after business."

Vital Signs

Stanley Marcus, as president of Neiman-Marcus, told salespeople in the Dallas store how to spot a potential sale: "As long as your customer is alive, you have a prospect."

People who sell show us how to open up communication, overcome obstacles, and get results, with humor power:

Today, Ira Hayes of Dayton, Ohio, is a well-known speaker. But he remembers when, some thirty years ago, he was a brand-new, nervous student salesman of cash registers. A seasoned pro took him into the territory. The pro didn't look like the movie version of a star salesman. He was short, chubby, red-faced. And brimming with humor power.

"In a small store, the owner abruptly declared, 'Not interested in no cash register,'" Ira says. "My associate leaned over on the counter and began chuckling as if he had just heard the world's funniest story. The store owner stared at him.

"My friend raised up, smiled, and apologized, 'I couldn't help laughing. You reminded me so much of another store owner who said he wasn't interested. Then he became one of my best customers.'

"This seasoned pro continued, seriously, with his sales presentation. Every time the store owner gave a reason for not being interested, my friend would put his head down on his arms and start that chuckling. He'd look up, then tell another story about someone who, after saying the very same thing, went for a new cash-register system.

"People were watching us. I was frozen with embarrassment—in fact, terrified," Ira admits. "I said to myself, 'They'll think we're a couple of nuts. We'll get thrown out of here.' The pro just kept chuckling, putting his head down, looking up —turning every objection the owner voiced into a humorous remembrance.

"In a surprisingly short time, we were carrying in a new cash register. My associate gave a thoughtful, professional demonstration—and the store owner bought the register!"

To this day, Ira Hayes tells us, "I can still see that chubby form, that smiling face, and hear that warm, meaningful chuckle. The memory has pulled me through many tough spots, by reminding me to put my humor power to work."

We can develop our humor-power resources with . . .

Proverbs for People Who Sell

* Great salesmen understand the value of prayer. They're used to keeping in touch with the home office.

* The greatest undeveloped territory is right under our hats.

* Think funny, and take the ice out of price. Help your cus-

tomer realize a dead battery is the only thing that's free of charge.

* Prospecting is like shaving. If a salesman doesn't do some, he'll look like a bum.

* The customer is always right. Misinformed, perhaps, inexact, bull-headed, fickle, even downright stupid—but never wrong.

* The emptier the pot, the quicker it boils. Watch your temper.

Even GBS had some winning advice for people who sell.

Do Not

Do not do unto others as you think they should do unto you. Their tastes may not be the same.

—GEORGE BERNARD SHAW

Draw on your humor-power resources, and you'll . . .

GAIN A WEALTH
OF VITAL ENERGY

Individuals who possess and use humor power lead many-faceted lives. They seem to overflow with the ability to act on their varied interests.

This wealth of vital energy built our nation. When America was young, our founders relied on humor power to help them cope with and conquer the terrors of the wilderness, the hardships of Colonial life, the challenge of a new land.

Remember Ben Franklin. His humor power lives for us in *Poor Richard's Almanac,* an annual collection of pithy proverbs. Poor Richard gave homely advice about going to bed early and saving pennies, but he also expressed himself in a manner akin to the modern one-liner:

Fish and guests smell after three days.
God heals, and the doctor takes the fee.

Blessed is the man who expects nothing; he shall never be disappointed.

With a wealth of vital energy, Ben Franklin put humor power to work. He succeeded—as a writer, printer, publisher, editor, scientist, inventor, general, statesman, diplomat, ambassador, and philosopher.

Yet Franklin's mother-in-law feared he couldn't support her daughter. He opened a print shop when there were already two printers in America. His mother-in-law worried that the nation wouldn't need a third!

She should have called on humor power. It banishes worries, relaxes tensions, and vanquishes fatigue. The humor-powered soon discover they can do more, more effectively.

Let's move forward in American history to the time when Thomas Alva Edison began his career as scientist, inventor, and businessman. Thanks to Edison, we have our modern electric lighting system, phonographs, dictating machines, and movies—to mention just a few benefits his vital energy gave *us*.

What's more, Edison was a humorist as well as a creator. His humor power gave *him* the energy to accomplish much— because he could think funny and take himself lightly. Here's just one example:

In childhood, Edison worked as a "candy butcher" selling candy, snacks, and newspapers on trains. An impatient conductor once pulled him on board by his ears—one explanation of why he became deaf in later years. But Edison could take his handicap lightly. With humor power, he claimed deafness shut out boring talk, so he could concentrate better.

And he also thought funny about ways to win, saying, "Everything comes to him who hustles while he waits."

When you think funny and take yourself lightly, you can
· · ·

Put Creativity to Work

Anxious, unsure individuals flypaper the rungs of the ladder to success with rules and regulations. They may acquire the power to control others and "lead" them to keep the rubber bands and paper clips in the neatest possible order. But they are likely to get tangled up on the way to meaningful goals. Creative thinking joins with humor power to lift real leaders above tangles and help them develop the leadership that inspires others.

Some people may look at creative ability from only one perspective. "Creativity means creating a great book, painting, musical composition, or sculpture. Or it may mean developing a great invention or scientific principle," they say, "but I can't do any of those things."

Actually, creativity can inspire achievement in every aspect of our personal and professional lives. We can even carry water in a sieve if we remember to freeze it first! And we can reach our goals with a creative approach that seeks answers, sometimes looks for discoveries through the glass of fantasy, and wonders, "What would happen if?"

Suppose, for instance, that your goal is to rid the world of mice. You're more likely to reach it if you forget about inventing a better mousetrap and seek another answer. From a humor-powered perspective, you might wonder, "What would happen if I fed my cat cheese? Then he could watch a mousehole with baited breath!"

Of course, you will recognize that feeding cheese to cats isn't the answer. But you can move ahead to another answer— because your think-funny perspective helps you accept yourself and your temporary setbacks.

The very best way to rid the world of mice has not yet been created. And, on our jobs, we haven't yet discovered the most effective way to conduct a meeting, write a letter, package a product, sell a service, or influence others. What's more, it's unlikely that we ever will find *the* best way—because individual moods, emotional climates, and situations vary. From the perspective of humor power, we can accept those variables and realize that fixed answers and attitudes are not effective, or even desirable.

It helps if we take ourselves and our job problems lightly.

An example from one of the world's great people makes the point:

When Albert Einstein was asked to explain his theory of relativity, he answered, "If you sit with a pretty girl for an hour, it seems like a minute. If you sit on a hot stove for a minute, it seems much longer than any hour. That's relativity!"

Although this example doesn't tell us the specific problems Einstein encountered as he developed his theory, it helps us understand his difficulties and his need to express his discovery in terms anyone could comprehend. That's creative communication!

In the business world, we can communicate better and achieve more by thinking funny and creatively. Consider this example:

Humor power burgeoned in the creative thinking of a graduate with obvious leadership potential. He dashed into a newspaper office and asked, "Need a good editor?"

"No."

"A reporter?"

"No."

"How about a copy boy?"

"No, we don't have any openings at the moment."

"Then you certainly need one of these." From his briefcase, the graduate produced a handsome sign lettered "No help wanted."

With humor power, creative thinking solves problems:

An examiner asked a police rookie, "How would you disperse a threatening mob?" The rookie considered the problem and decided, "I'd start taking up a collection."

Creativity, powered by humor, can help us become more flexible in our approach to our jobs. In turn, flexibility promotes the give-and-gain attitude we need for success. We can help others accept us and our leadership. Acceptance results when we apply humor power to say, "I don't feel self-important, but I do feel self-confident about my creative achievements." For example:

From today's vantage point, we know that Michael Faraday's invention of the dynamo led onward to achievements by others. In fact, this first dynamo fathered much of our modern technology. But, in Faraday's lifetime, some persons didn't see the importance of his invention.

When one individual belittled him by asking, "What good is a dynamo?" Faraday responded, humor-powerfully but seriously, "What good is a baby?"

Now, let's examine the same approach from an on-the-job perspective:

In a candy store, one salesclerk always had customers lined up waiting to buy from her, though other clerks might be standing around, bored and discontented because they had nothing to do. The store owner asked the first salesclerk, "What's your secret?"

"Simple," she replied. "Other clerks scoop up more than a pound of candy and then start taking candy away. I always scoop up less than a pound and then add to it."

With humor power, this salesclerk showed that she had a success-oriented picture of herself, respected her own ability to create sales, and didn't need to boast.

A top award for humor-powered creativity might go to the bus driver who solved a persistent problem. "Everybody with clean underwear move to the back of the bus," he hollered. "The rest with dirty underwear, stay up here with me." And passengers thronged to the back of the bus!

When you and your job don't fit, you can admit it—with creative humor power:

Applying for a job, a recent graduate was given an aptitude test. When he came to the question "What does 'cryogenics' mean?" he paused and puzzled over it. At last, the graduate wrote, "It means I'd better look somewhere else for a job."

Try, Try

If at first you don't succeed, try, try again. Then quit. There's no use being a damn fool about it.

—W. C. FIELDS

But do make certain you first try harder:

I am only an average man, but, by George, I work
harder at it than the average man.

—THEODORE ROOSEVELT

HOMEMAKERS' HOW-TO

"You're looking unusually cheerful this evening, dear. Are you
winning the rat race?"

Nowadays, more husbands are asking that question of
their wives, as more and more women join the work force—
where, of course, they want to work for equal pay.

"Equal pay makes sense," a friend told me. "If a woman
works like a horse, naturally she should be paid like a man."

One of the great things about human liberation is that it
gives a woman the freedom to select homemaking as her top-
priority job. Rosalyn Sussman Yalow, however, maintains she
wanted everything—marriage and a career—and got it. She's a
Bronx homemaker, mother, physicist—and Nobel Prize winner.

If you define your job as "housewife," "homemaker,"
"secretary of the interior," or, perhaps, "spousekeeper," you
need help to cope. And if you combine homemaking with another job, this need escalates. More help is yours, with humor
power.

You thought you were an equal partner, but the door-to-
door salesman asks, "Is the head of the house at home?" Slam
the door! Or, try the humor-powered solution. "Sorry, but he's
in kindergarten just now."

Your friendly neighbor drops in—frequently. Her little
drop-ins add up to mighty oceans of wasted time for you. A
homemaker tells me this creative idea works:

Answer the door with your coat on. If it's your neighbor,
or anyone else you don't want to see, say, "Sorry, I was just

leaving," and enjoy a walk around the block. If you have time for a visitor, exclaim, "Glad you caught me! I just got in."

You're a busy mother—and Dad brings home a puppy. While the kids are deciding what to call it, tell them, "You'd better call it 'Mother,' because if that dog stays, I'm leaving."

You're "moonlighting" at a part- or full-time job, and you need help with your primary job of homemaking. Enlighten your husband about doing his share. This story could help.

The street was quiet, except for an angry voice coming from one house. A man shouted, "I demand some consideration! Show your respect for me. Get me plenty of hot water. I'm not going to wash dishes in cold water for any woman."

Your single friends think you gave up your liberty in pursuit of happiness. Let them know you take pride in your job. After all, no other career could give you the opportunity to display your talents as maintenance engineer, chef, child-development expert, hostess, nurse, purchasing agent, supplies manager, couturière, decorator, chauffeur, dog walker—and to have ulcers and humor power, too!

APPRECIATE OTHERS
—Laugh with Them

Unless we can appreciate the contribution that the humor power of others makes to our development, it's probably impossible for us to motivate others with our humor power. We can show we value the bonus others give us by laughing with them.

Signs deliver the bonus. With other factors equal, a couple might choose the obstetrician whose welcome mat says "THIS is where you come when you're through playing games." Food seems to taste better in a restaurant with the sign "No checks. We have several from last year."

Humor power can give and gain recognition of an in-common problem, with the bonus of empathy for others' perspectives. This happens when the sign on the trash-removal truck reads "Satisfaction guaranteed, or double your garbage back."

Perhaps the most important thing that others do for us with their humor-powered examples is to help us relieve job-related tensions, chase frustration, and cope with problems. Remember, the only person with his problems behind him is a school-bus driver.

The Loizeaux family specializes in the serious, and dangerous, job of demolishing buildings and other structures with explosives. Understandably, on-the-job tension runs high. The Loizeauxs relieve it with humor power—often by telling tall tales to local reporters. Before one big demolition job, a newspaper reporter asked them what they would do about flying dust and debris.

"We had a huge Baggie custom-made by the Baggies sandwich-bag people," Doug Loizeaux explained solemnly. "Helicopters will drop it over the building."

The reporter fell for the put-on. And the Loizeauxs released tension with gales of laughter as they read the story in the newspaper.

Tall tales can chase frustration, too, by enhancing the value of our jobs—in a playful manner. Two insurance men illustrated that point when they exchanged brags about how fast their firms paid off claims. Nine times out of ten, the first man claimed, his firm had a check in the policyholder's hands on the very day an accident happened.

"That's nothing," scoffed the second man. "Our offices are on the twenty-third floor of the Lee Building. It's forty stories high. Just the other day, one of our policyholders jumped off the roof of the building. As he passed the twenty-third floor, we handed him his check."

By kidding others and laughing with them, we give. In fact, we can give what most people want most from their jobs —a more relaxed, more open, sharing attitude.

Give-and-Gain—
Share Laughter

On your job, you can help others laugh about the funny things they unconsciously do:

Tell the story of the bus repairman who filled out a report on a highway accident. When he came to the section "Disposition of Passengers" he wrote, "Mad as hell!"

Or, you may want your kidding to involve an office problem:

Tell the story about the personnel manager who filled in a questionnaire. One question asked, "How many people do you have working in your company, broken down by sex?" His answer: "Liquor is more of a problem with us."

Better still, laugh at yourself:

Tell either of those two stories and apply it to your own behavior—to open up about the funny things *you* unconsciously do. In addition, you can use the experiences of the bus repairman or the personnel manager to illustrate the difficulty of communicating, or to reinforce the point that there are many ways of looking at and solving specific problems.

Let me offer some examples of two-way giving and gaining through shared laughter.

You and your boss gain when he laughs at himself and with you, and you return the compliment. He might say, "Don't think of me as your boss. Just think of me as a friend who's always right." And you might reply, "Actually, I think of you as a jigsaw puzzle—when you try to solve a problem, you go to pieces."

Through shared laughter, you can smooth relationships with others who are trying to do their jobs right. For example:

You, to your letter carrier: "I see spring is a little late this year. The postal service must be delivering it."

Your letter carrier, to you: "Don't worry. We're working on a way to deliver old age by mail."

You, to your physician: "I know you're a very successful doctor—so successful that if a patient doesn't have anything wrong with him, you will tell him so."

Your physician, to you: "I'm successful because I'm a specialist. That means I've trained my patients to become ill during office hours."

You, to your auto mechanic: "I saw an ad in the paper and it said, 'Mechanic wanted. Must *look* honest.'"

Your auto mechanic, to you: "I'll *be* honest. I really like the fabric upholstery in your car. It's lots better than leather or vinyl—for wiping my hands on."

You, to an on-the-job associate: "Well, I see you know the secret of doing your job right. And you know how to keep it a secret."

Your associate, to you: "Thanks for giving me a piece of your mind. I appreciate it—especially when your inventory is so low."

Sometimes, it pays to . . .

Squeak a Little

Overheard at the water cooler: "His feelings are hurt. He had to travel tourist on the company plane."

This legendary business traveler may have had reason to gripe about his hurt feelings. At times, all of us need to be more assertive in our job relationships. If that's the case with you, remember which wheel gets the grease. Squeak a little, with humor power.

You may hesitate to complain, even about an obvious problem, because you have your own version of the theatrical motto "The show must go on." Keep your show going, but recognize the moment when it's time to complain. Squeak up . . .

When others unjustly criticize you.

At the company cafeteria, employees constantly criticized the food—and the food-service director. He reacted by applying the half-sting of humor power:

"The Bible tells us that Jesus Christ fed the multitudes with five loaves and two fishes. This was called a miracle. But some people think a miracle means a food-service director of a company cafeteria."

When others prevent you from doing your job right.

One evening on the bus, a woman pestered the driver, reminding him every block or two where she wanted to get off. He listened patiently until she wailed, "But how will I know when I get to my stop?" Said the bus driver, "By the big smile on my face, lady."

When others aren't doing their jobs right.

A diner said to the waiter, "What's our offense? We've been on bread and water for more than an hour."

And if *you* need humor power to improve your associates' on-the-job attitudes, you could make your point by telling about the bus driver's answer, the diner's quip, or by using any of the following examples.

When others expect too much and make too many demands.

A film star nagged Alfred Hitchcock about camera angles. Again and again, she told him to make sure she was photographed from "my best side." "Sorry, can't be done," Hitchcock said. "We can't photograph you from your best side. You're sitting on it."

Or: "Last night I called my doctor at three A.M. and said I hated to bother him, but I had a bad case of insomnia."

"What are you trying to do," he asked, "start an epidemic?"

When others don't deliver as expected.

Comedian and singer Eddie Cantor appeared at a veterans hospital where he worked hard to make the patients laugh. Closing the show, he said, "Hope you're better soon, fellows."

Chorused the veterans, "Same to you!"

When others show they're pompous and puffed up.

The major snapped at the PFC, "In civilian life you wouldn't come to me with a silly complaint like this."

"No, sir," agreed the PFC. "I'd send for you."

When others ask for your opinion, and it's unfavorable.

Express your judgment honestly, but with humor power.

Sam Goldwyn accompanied a producer to a preview of a blood-and-thunder epic. After the film, the producer demanded, "Now, isn't that a real swashbuckler?"

"Yes," Goldwyn said, "but the trouble is, it buckles where it should swash."

When things go wrong, squeak up! When things go right, keep on doing what you're doing. And remember, silence solves problems, too. Squeak up to be heard, shut up to be appreciated!

MANAGE THE BOSS—
It's the American Way!

Company president, department manager, foreman, group leader, project head, or anyone in a leadership role, "the boss" is a natural target for humor power. In fact, "kidding the boss" has become an American tradition, as our habit of laughing with our political leaders shows.

"You have to admire the straightforward way the candidate is dodging the issues," we may say. Or: "Have you noticed that recently the President seems to be taking his job very seriously? And why not? He wants to be right up there with the other biggies. Andrew Johnson, Zachary Taylor, and Millard Fillmore."

Our Presidents have been kidded for everything from their personalities to their policies and achievements. In a serious but humor-powered toast, Ben Franklin said that George Washington, as general of the army, "like Joshua of old, commanded the sun and the moon to stand still, and they obeyed him."

Calvin Coolidge was kidded for his silence and reserve. "If you don't say anything, then you don't have to repeat it," he said. Back in 1926, "Silent Cal" went to see *The Coconuts*, starring the Marx brothers, at Washington's National Theatre. Most cast members were awed by the President's presence. Not Groucho Marx.

Groucho stopped in the middle of a comic song, pranced to the footlights, peered out at the audience, and demanded, "Calvin, aren't you up beyond your bedtime?"

When a conservative industrialist visited John F. Kennedy in the White House, JFK told him, "If I weren't President, I would buy stocks now."

The industrialist nodded. "If you weren't President, so would I."

Today's business leaders come in for their share of kidding. The leader with humor power accepts and returns the kidding. After all, the rat race isn't so bad when you're a big cheese! Most bosses appreciate being kidded; they recognize that kidding equals liking. For example, the "roast," to honor a leader in almost any field. Typical quips might include:

"The things my boss does for his employees can be counted on his little finger."

"He had to work hard to get where he is. *His* boss didn't have a daughter."

"They kid the boss too much. They kid about his looks, they kid about his personality. I don't. I don't think he has any."

Kidding your boss can help you manage your job relationships more effectively—with your boss and with other associates.

That's why one executive said to another, "The boss calls it delegating authority, but I call it passing the buck."

Some employees feel sorry for the boss. He's the one who has to watch the clock at coffee breaks, and the one who gets up early to see who comes in late.

After her first day on the job, the new secretary reported, "My boss is mean, but he's fair. He's mean to everybody."

When you ask for a raise, laugh at yourself and with your boss. "I've got my shoulder to the wheel, my nose to the grindstone, and I'm going broke. Who can work in that position?" A humor-powered boss might surprise you by replying, "All right, I'll give you a raise—a nice big one. I want your last two weeks here to be happy ones."

Remember, a kidding approach often means the opposite

of what it seems to say. That's how to brag about your staff, your assistant, or your boss!

"It isn't true my boss is a workaholic. He never touches the stuff."

"The boss gave me the day off for my golden wedding anniversary. He's generous. Just said he hopes I won't keep bothering him for time off every fifty years."

"Our boss is a real motivator. He motivates us to get to work on time—by providing fifty parking spaces for seventy-five employees."

"My boss is a big deal in the business world. Anytime anyone mentions his name, they say, 'Big deal!' "

With humor power, you can show you're loyal to your boss, even though you may disagree with him.

When the late Hubert H. Humphrey was Vice-President during Texan Lyndon B. Johnson's presidency, some critics thought he should speak out loudly when he disagreed with Johnson.

Kansas Citian Chris Bowker values the memory of a Humphrey press conference he attended as a teen-ager interested in government and politics. Reporters hurled questions at the Vice-President, hoping to stir up controversy. He could have responded with a curt "No comment." Instead, Chris recalls, Humphrey smilingly replied, to each controversial question, "The eyes of Texas are upon me."

You're the Boss

Laugh at yourself when others apply the needle and you can demonstrate the humor power that those who lead others must have. But laughing at yourself does *not* mean focusing on yourself. Invite others to laugh with you in a way that focuses on them. You'll generate the humor power that leads through motivation.

"I see the sales charts just hit new highs. I looked at them upside down."

Or: "My new secretary says I'm sort of bigoted. I insist words should always be spelled the same way."

Whatever you do with your humor power, don't work for or expect a continual chorus of laughs and smiles from those you lead. You might learn to be a stand-up comedian, but you wouldn't become outstanding as a humor-powered motivator.

Here's a real-life illustration.

Jack T. of St. Louis explains why today he works in a library instead of a newspaper office. Early in his working life, he held a job on a farm news weekly.

"My boss, the publisher, was one of the world's great humorists," Jack says. "At least, he was, to hear him tell it—and he did tell it, or any joke, over and over again. For instance, he put up a suggestion box in the office, mostly to have something to tell jokes about. But he liked his own jokes so much, he often lost the humor in a long buildup.

"He would open the box, talking continuously. 'This is a fine suggestion box, made of the best knotty pine. You can tell it's knotty pine by the holes. You can see the hole show. But there's no hole in the bottom. You can't see the floor show.'

"We were expected to smile, not laugh, during the buildup. When he was ready to tell the joke, he would take a sheet of paper out of the box and pretend to read it. Some of his jokes were funny, or would have been, if he had told them simply. I remember once he pretended to read an employee's suggestion, frowned, and said, 'I don't understand. Can't you be more specific? What kind of kite? What lake?'

"Immediately, he stepped on the point. 'Get it? I'm saying the suggestion told me to go fly a kite, to go jump in the lake. Get it?' Then, and only then, he paused and waited for us to laugh.

"We couldn't help laughing at his jokes, not if we wanted to keep our jobs. Finally," Jack concludes, "I got the point. I couldn't take one more 'funny' routine, so I quit laughing, and quit my job. Did anyone ever put a suggestion in that box? I doubt it."

When you focus your humor power on your associates, you have the option to roast *them* a little. Like the boss who told the computer salesman, "Show me something small. I just want to replace one smart aleck."

Or the boss who said to his executive assistant, "Must you concentrate all your imagination, initiative, and daring on your expense account?"

Your efficient secretary will appreciate being kidded, thanks to the compliment implied by opposites, when you tell someone else, "I don't know about her typing speed, but she can erase thirty-three words a minute."

Let your humor power demonstrate your creative behavior.

The president of a firm showed a friend through the offices —including several small, private rooms. In each one sat a young man, earnestly typing. When the friend asked about the young men, the boss explained, "Those are some of our junior executives."

"Then why are they typing letters?"

"I know what I'm doing," the boss replied. "I can hire a junior executive for half the salary I'd have to pay a stenographer!"

But the most important reason for improving leader-to-associate relationships is this:

Every manager and leader delegates his future to his associates.

When you apply humor power to help others achieve more, you'll find it easier to delegate not just responsibility but options for creative initiative. And humor power can improve your future—because your associates will identify with you, thanks to your ability to open up, share laughter, think funny, and take yourself lightly.

Take Risks, Early

In your on-the-job relationships, be the first to take the risk of showing your associates that you're human and sometimes goof. Let humor power reveal your flaws, your inconsistencies, your mistakes.

Why do I keep repeating that you and I do make mistakes?

The greatest of faults is to be conscious of none.

—THOMAS CARLYLE

Revealing our faults and mistakes leads to self-knowledge, which, in turn, generates self-confidence. Sometimes, we don't know our real capabilities until we see and admit we have goofed.

Consider this example, from the experience of a mythical individual who was job hunting. When he was told that the job he sought was a very responsible position, he piped up, "I'm just the person you want. On my last job, every time something went wrong, they said I was responsible."

Although this response won't help him at the moment, it may open up an opportunity—to see himself, realize that he does make mistakes, and admit it. And that's the first move on the way to a stronger self-image plus an improved performance.

When we take the risk of admitting mistakes, it's the safe thing to do. People will be less critical, because we've humanized ourselves and their view of us.

Take risks early, to establish your reputation as a humor-powered communicator and motivator. You'll give more of yourself away and gain in the process. You can gain the ability to do the toughest of all jobs—getting others to accept change.

Yes, it *is* tough. When change sweeps through a company, departments may be reorganized, job descriptions revised, and individual responsibilities increased or diminished. The very fact of change is unsettling, and individuals may resist *any* change in their on-the-job responsibilities.

While humor power can't produce immediate contentment, it will help you influence others to accept change. In part, you can do this by approaching the problem from a think-funny perspective. For instance, you might say:

"Times have changed. Years ago, we used to hide our family skeletons in closets. Now, we let them parade around in bikinis."

But change will become more acceptable if you can recommend it on the basis of your established image as a trustworthy individual. Remember, "I like you" leads to "I understand you" and on to "I believe you." And the goal you gain is trust. Risk a little and gain a lot by applying humor power—to show you're human, likable, believable, and trustworthy.

Humor power engenders a relaxed, comfortable exchange, a dialogue conducted in a friendly and inviting manner. Here's a true-to-life example, with the facts changed slightly to protect the humor-powered.

The advertising department of a large firm brought in a new, young creative director. An older man was transferred to a subordinate position. During their first business conversation, the young director felt nervous in his new role and embarrassed about giving orders to the older man. He took the risk, with humor power.

"As Walter Winchell used to say," he assured his older colleague, "we'll get along scrappily ever after." His colleague nodded. "We're going to make some changes," the director continued. "We don't want to give boredom a bad name. Winchell used to say that, too."

"I see," said the colleague.

Curious about his lack of reaction, the director asked, "You *have* heard of Walter Winchell? The famous columnist? The one who went into broadcasting, back in the thirties?"

"Sure," said the older man, accepting change with humor power. "My father told me about him."

Humor power has a way of making your point effectively even when you think your associate or customer may have missed it. It seems to exert a subliminal force.

Another example from Kansas Citian Chris Bowker illustrates this—with an assist from "Camptown Races."

A few years ago, Chris helped a friend who owned a tavern by occasionally tending bar. One night a customer reeled in, loaded with liquor and potential trouble.

Leaning on the bar, he asked, "Do the Main Street buses run all night?"

Solemnly, Chris answered, "Doodah, doodah."

The man wove his way to a second bartender. "Shay, do the Main Street buses run all night?"

With equal solemnity, that bartender said, "Doodah, doodah."

More befuddled than ever, the man tried to focus, shrugged, and lurched back into the night, taking trouble away. While he didn't see the joke, he did get the message—because the two bartenders modified their own moods through humor power and handled a bothersome situation in a lighthearted way.

Humor power puts the message across and gets results.

7 Put Your Message Across with Humor Power

During his first night on duty, the new guard at the prison was surprised by the cheerful atmosphere and puzzled to hear the inmates calling numbers from cell to cell. "Thirteen!" "Forty-six!" "Twenty-two!" After each number, roars of laughter rocked the cell block.

An experienced guard joined in. "Seventy-seven!" he hollered, and sure enough, the inmates laughed.

"What's with the numbers?" the new guard asked.

"These prisoners know their favorite jokes so well, they've numbered them," the other guard explained. "That way, they can just give a number to get a laugh."

When his second night on duty arrived, the new guard moistened his lips, cleared his throat, and shouted, "Fifty-seven!"

The cell block was silent. Not a single laugh sounded.

Embarrassed, the new guard asked, "What's wrong? I gave a number, like everyone else. Why didn't they laugh?"

"That's the way it goes," the experienced guard replied. "Some people just can't tell a joke."

When I talk with individuals from my audiences, they tell me they have the same problem. They know the value of humor in making points to another individual, two or three persons, or a larger group, and they wish they could tell jokes more effectively.

If you think you can't tell a joke, ask yourself two questions.

1. Are you limiting yourself to only one form of joke? Most of us tend to think of a joke as a story or an anecdote, with a scene to set, a situation to describe, and a punch line in conclusion. Don't overlook the impact of brief humor. Remember the aphorism, the quip, the one-liner. They're jokes, too. One of Henny Youngman's famous one-liners is known as the world's shortest joke: "Take my wife—please!"

President Coolidge, "Silent Cal," made words count. When he was asked what a minister who preached about sin had said, Silent Cal replied, "He was against it."

Some one-liners may have two or three lines, but still they're as short and power-packed as many a punch line for a longer story. "When labor leader George Meany told a bedtime story to his grandchildren, he always started it, 'Once upon a time-and-a-half.'"

One-liners, quips, and aphorisms carry points. They can help you convey yours to people who think they don't have time to listen.

2. Are you sure you should be "telling jokes"? Use humor, of course, but take advantage of the truth that there's more to humor power than jokes. Perhaps quiet, thoughtful humor, the kind that doesn't strive for belly laughs, is best suited to your personality.

Search

When a thing is funny, search it for a hidden truth.

—GEORGE BERNARD SHAW

Humor's power has depth, seeks out truth, lies hidden until your attitude reveals it. It can come through in simple words. For example, a question popped up in my business correspondence.

"Can you *humor me* on this?" a letter asked. I found myself smiling, ready to give a yes answer. The expression "humor me" put me "in humor."

My correspondent was Morrie E. Halvorsen, executive director of a distributors' association headquartered in Elm Grove, Wisconsin. Morrie had invited me to keynote a sales meeting, and he asked me to "humor him" by making a change in props for my presentation. The details of the change aren't important here, but this is:

With gentle humor power directed toward himself, he persuaded me to do what he wanted, not because he wanted me to do it, but because I now wanted to do it. That's motivation!

In our personal, social, family, and job lives, it's our privilege to humor others. We empathize with their thoughts and wishes. We make our own points by accepting theirs. If we're out of humor, we're cross, displeased, dissatisfied, and others react crossly to us. Humor power depends on our being "in humor," filled with warmth and good nature, not merely on being funny.

The "how" of being funny can't be pinpointed precisely, measured and weighed, or created by formula. A gallon of humor won't produce a predictable smileage. Who would want it to? Humor equals fun because it's unpredictable.

You can generate humor power by combining "who" and "Why." "Who" is you and your way of being warm, good-natured, and, at times, funny. "Why" is your reason for exercising humor power—to *communicate* your message, make it *memorable,* and make others *eager to act* on it. What's the message? It's any idea, suggestion, or strategy you want to put across. From "who" and "why," "how" is yours when you convert your sense of humor into humor power, make ripples by spreading your humor power, and make others happy by attacking their judgment!

Convert your sense of humor into authentic humor power.

To me, a sense of humor is an ability to see the light side. It's joyful, comes easily, is not particularly planned. This sense stems from the feeling of being "in fun" and grows to be almost intuitive. In relation to humor power, it could be compared to a diesel engine. We have to get the little motor going before the big one will work. Like most powers, humor power is learned, then applied, and you have to work at it first!

Example: Steve, one of my sons, teaches tennis. He applies humor power, working at it with children under six. He has the children call the tennis racquet a "lollipop": "Hold your lollipop higher."

It works! "Racquet" is a hard word for little kids to remember, but "lollipop" is memorable. One child will say to another, "John, do you have your lollipop?"

To an adult, Steve says, "Turn sideways to the net." To a child, he says, "Point your belly button to the post."

Memorable! Work at *your* humor power, and help others remember your messages.

Make ripples—spread your humor power.

Toss a pebble in a pool, and the ripples spread out. Humor power works, when you work at it, in the same manner.

Example: Mack McGinnis, humor services editor, developed an experiment to explore how humor power spreads. It's an experiment you can try.

"I've done short research with a joke which I would tell to a friend upon entering the building where I work," Mack explains. "Frequently, when leaving the building to go home that evening, I would have the same joke told to me—by a different person, of course, and in a different way, but with the same general elements.

"During the day, I can only guess how many smiles that one bit of humor triggered as it was relayed to others in that building. And the point is that one humor bit helped each person who told it improve his personal public relations."

Amuse others by attacking their judgment with ridiculous but convincing opposites. Humor power is based on opposites, but simple opposites aren't automatically funny. "Night and day" or "solid pebbles and liquid pools" will not result in laughter, for the same reason the contrast between a high note and a low note struck on a piano doesn't result in broken sobs. Some creative composition is needed.

For humor power, the composition begins with an attack on your listener's judgment. Attack with enough exaggeration to make extreme opposites convincing. "Enough" means "not much," for you need only convince the subconscious mind, and the subconscious isn't too critical.

Example: Oscar Wilde created convincing, and witty, opposites. He wrote such things as "He's old enough to know worse"; "I do not approve of anything that tampers with natural ignorance"; "A gentleman is someone who is never unintentionally rude"; and "One can always be kind to people about whom one cares nothing."

Wilde's exaggerated opposites sound all right to the subconscious mind, until the conscious mind examines their incongruity more carefully.

The more extreme the exaggeration, the more it approaches the opposite of your listener's beliefs. The greater the extreme, the stronger and funnier, provided you make the exaggeration convincing for the short time it takes listeners to reject the attack, see the point, and laugh.

Exaggerations grow progressively funnier as they approach the greatest believable extreme. Beyond that extreme, they aren't funny.

Example: When an artist caricatures a large nose, he makes it larger. Whatever humor there is in a nose becomes greater as the nose becomes larger—until it reaches the point where a viewer is totally unconvinced that such a nose could exist. The viewer's judgment is no longer attacked, so there is nothing to reject. A nose that extends all the way across a room has no humor at all! Exaggerate, but be believable.

COMMUNICATE
YOUR MESSAGE, CLEARLY

Applied as a communications system, humor power does more than release tensions and evaporate hostility. It opens up channels to others, shows us how to communicate clearly, and reminds us when we aren't communicating.

We aren't—unless we listen to what others say. Let attention wander, and a half-heard comment thoroughly confuses us. That's why some people think "copper nitrate" is a police officer's overtime pay!

We also don't communicate unless we make certain what we say or show means the same thing to another individual.

A police officer stopped a senior citizen who breezed past him in her car while he was directing traffic. "Madam," he asked, "didn't you see my hand raised? Don't you know what that means?"

"Yes, of course I do," she retorted. "I taught school for forty years."

Hell?

Commenting on his "Give 'em hell, Harry" reputation, President Truman said, "I never give them hell. I just tell the truth, and they think it's hell."

After a secretary had made several mistakes, in an absent-minded way, her boss asked, "Are you in love?"

"Of course not," she snapped. "I'm married."

At a sidewalk cafe in Paris, the artist James Whistler went to the rescue of some American tourists who seemed to be having trouble communicating their order to a waiter. The tourists told him, angrily, "We speak French. We don't need help."

"Oh, sorry," said Whistler. "I thought I heard you tell the waiter to serve you a flight of steps."

We communicate with clarity when we put humor power to work. Carl Winters, a Chicago-based speaker and clergyman, comments, "I make my congregation laugh, and while their mouths are open, I put in something for them to chew on."

Here's one of Carl's favorite point-making stories:

Little Jimmie, five years old, was watching his minister put some names over the altar in preparation for a service on Sunday. "Reverend Jones," he asked, "who are those people? Why are you putting their names up?"

"Those are the names of people who died in the service."

Jimmie thought for a while and then said, "Which service, Mr. Jones, the nine-thirty or the eleven o'clock?"

Wherever there's a message about communication, there's a quip or vignette to illustrate it.

"My doctor told me to eat more leafy greens," the fellow said, "so I've switched from martinis to mint juleps."

Mama Mouse was taking her children for a stroll across the kitchen floor when a cat suddenly appeared. "Bow wow!" barked Mama Mouse. "Woof! Grr! Bow wow!" The confused cat ran away, and the mouse said to her children, "You see, I was right when I told you it pays to know a second language."

When a wealthy woman commissioned her portrait, she asked the artist, "Do you object to painting me in the nude?"

"Not at all," said the artist, "if you'll let me keep my socks on. I must have someplace to put my brushes."

If we would rather not communicate in response to a personal or prying question, humor power can put that message across, too.

NEIGHBOR: Robert doesn't look as well dressed as he did back when you two got married.

WIFE: That's strange. I'm sure he's wearing the same suit.

The subject of age doesn't wear well, either. "If they try to discover when I was born," reports actress/comedienne Imogene Coca, "I always say 1492."

When Churchill was interviewed on his eighty-seventh

birthday, a young reporter said, "Sir Winston, I hope to wish you well on your one-hundredth birthday."

Churchill responded, "You might do it. You look healthy."

An inquisitive fan asked humorist Steve Allen, "Do you wear a toupee?"

"The hair is real," Steve confided. "It's the head that's fake."

To another real-or-false question, Al Robertson, a retired Missouri businessman, applied the bite of humor power. "Sure, I have all my own teeth," he replied. "I paid for them."

More often, though, you'll be interested in communicating as much as you can, as forcefully and clearly as possible.

1. Watch Your Language—Try the KISS System

Suppose Josh wants to make a good impression at a social, civic, or business gathering. He decides to express his message, and his humor power, with dignity, formality, and jawbreaking words.

"It is incumbent upon me," intones Jawbreaker Josh, "to apprise this assemblage that every vicissitude is endowed with amusingness, insofar as the specified circumstance is transpiring in the embodiment of another personage."

Will Rogers said it simply: "Everything is funny as long as it's happening to somebody else."

Somewhere in a tangle of syllables, Josh lost his message. That won't happen to you and me, if we count on the KISS system.

KISS began as a bridge joke. At the bridge table, it stands for "Keep It Super Simple." (I refuse to agree with my partners that when I'm playing bridge it means, "Keep It Simple, Stupid!") For communicating and motivating, keep your language simple, active, and direct. Amuse, but don't confuse. KISS, and make your message easy to understand. In any language, even simple words can trap communicators. Get fancy or go pompous, and communication gets harder.

Time to Conquer

The Romans would never have found time to conquer the world if they had been obliged to learn Latin first.

—HEINRICH HEINE

Humorous goofs remind us to watch our words and make their meaning exact. *Unlike* the sign in the window of a New York drugstore: "Why pay more elsewhere?" Or the night-club sign: "Good clean entertainment every night except Sunday." Or the ad: "Now you can have a girdle for a ridiculous figure."

Quip, kid, and convey your message in a natural, conversational manner. If you're comfortable with expressive slang, use it. But *handle dialect with care*—which usually means don't use it. It's difficult to put across, and it's an old-fashioned form of humor that may strike others as a put-down.

Be careful about using words from foreign languages, even though you speak another language, or several, with fluency. You may block communication because others don't understand and feel shut out. Or, they may understand too well, spotting mistakes.

Ray Monsalvatge, a multilingual speaker, once gave me an unusual example of communicating in a foreign language with unintentional humor. Although he used a Spanish word correctly, he wasn't aware the word had developed a special connotation.

"Speaking to an audience of two thousand women at the University of Puerto Rico, I tried to tell of a six-year-old girl who had been humiliated," Ray told me. "I used the perfectly good Spanish word for 'embarrassed,' which is *'embarasada.'*

"The whole auditorium cracked up, with uproarious laughter. I didn't know why until after the speech. That word is currently used only as slang for 'pregnant.'"

Groucho Marx wrote to William Scranton, then governor of Pennsylvania, to correct his pronunciation of a Yiddish word. Groucho's message was, "When you campaign in Jewish neighborhoods, rhyme mishmash with slosh."

Don't be too careful! Use words to create effective images. Think funny, in three dimensions and in living color.

When he was asked how well he knew General Douglas MacArthur, President Eisenhower created a colorful character sketch. "I knew him well," he quipped. "I studied dramatics under him for fourteen years."

2.   Compare, and Count to Three

Humor power works by comparison, or simile, as well as by contrast. Compare, and make your messages come alive with clarity. Study these samples:

Husbands are like fires. They go out when unattended.

—ZSA ZSA GABOR

A kiss is like a rumor. It goes from mouth to mouth.

—*Godey's Lady's Book*

Conscience is like a baby. It has to go to sleep before you can.

Some people are like tea bags. They don't know their own strength until they get into hot water.

Doing business without advertising is like winking at a woman in the dark.

Playing golf is like raising kids. You keep hoping you're going to do better.

Don't insult his intelligence. That would be like a mercy killing.

Young adults are a little like gardens. Beautiful to behold, if nurtured. Like a tangle of weeds, if left to grow as best they can.

If you eliminate the "like" in the comparison, you form a metaphor and communicate even more vividly. A tennis racquet, to little kids, isn't "like" a lollipop—it *is* one.

Speaking of cities and highways, sociologist Lewis Mumford reinforced his message with: "Our national flower is the concrete cloverleaf."

Metaphors can express messages satirically. Glenn Gould, Canadian musician and writer, parodied a familiar saying when he wrote, "Behind every silver lining, there's a cloud."

Try another effective pattern for humor power. Count to three! Or, build up to a point, with sayings in three.

Three things a man never gets back. Youth, his hair, and change from a ten-dollar bill.

If you're retired, and you worry about Social Security going broke, don't worry. If you're retired, and you hear about Social Security paying out more than it's taking in, don't worry. But if you're retired, and your Social Security check is postdated—worry!

3.   Be Timely—Don't Be Dated

"No, dumb Dora, that doesn't mean be on time for dates or you won't have any."

That's an example of what I mean, and a horrible example at that. Put-down quips about women's intelligence have never communicated humor power, and today they're totally out of date. Humor and communication bomb when a joke is dated and out of tune with the times.

In Fashion?

"There are fashions in jokes as in clothes," wrote Robert Lynd, British humorist. "The clothes of fifty years ago seem comic to us. The jokes of fifty years ago . . . do not."

Life-styles change and jokes fade from funny to pointless. This one is fading: "Will you give me a penny, mister? I haven't eaten for three days, and I want to weigh myself." Its point is blunted, as the weight-for-a-penny scale vanishes. It may return, in a new form, if another coin begins to equal "weigh" and "scale" in our minds.

A few individuals have possessed the rare ability to make their humor timeless. Their sayings appear again and again, always apt, appropriate, and apt to be appropriated!

Often, an example of humor power will be credited to not one but two famous persons. It isn't easy to know which one first quipped the quip, carved the satirical point, or experienced the moment of gently amusing insight. Not when both are noted for their humor power!

Will Rogers—you've met him!—and Dizzy Dean, 1930s St. Louis Cardinals pitcher and sportscaster, have been credited with this comment, made when Will's, or Dizzy's, grammar was criticized: "Maybe ain't ain't so correct, but I notice a lotta fellers who ain't sayin' ain't, ain't eatin'."

A point-making anecdote has been told about Edison—and about Einstein. Edison or Einstein was attending either a dull social gathering or a dull scientific meeting. To Edison or Einstein, a sympathetic person said, "You must be very bored."

"Oh, no," replied the famous man. "At times like these, I retire to the back of my mind, and there I am always amused."

Usually humor about current events is highly perishable— funny only until we go on to the next event. Will Rogers proved some refreshing exceptions to that rule.

"The country is prosperous on the whole," he said, "but how much prosperity is there in a hole?" And: "Politics has got so expensive, it takes lots of money to even get beat with." In the next presidential election, he joked, he would not run— "no matter how much the country may need a comedian by then."

Use topical humor, of course. It's vital, anytime you want to lift the load with laughter. Be alert, though, for the moment when "here and now" humor becomes yesterday's old story. Fortunately for all of us, times change, and changes affect the impact of vignettes like this one:

"Morton drove home in a Toyota, took off his Hong Kong suit, shut off the Taiwan stereo, turned on the Japanese television, and was surprised to hear the U.S. trade deficit was at an all-time high."

Chances are, humor about taxes will always offer a fresh way to communicate—because humor power answers the need to think funny about painful reality. "Did you notice on the new IRS form it says, 'Item A: How much did you make last year? Item B: Send Item A.'"

"When you sit down to figure out your income tax, remember the tax collector's three R's. This is ours, that is ours, everything is ours."

"The new tax forms take a realistic approach. In front of the space where your spouse signs, they say, 'Accomplice.'"

Communicators take note. Humor can age fast, yet freshness is vital to its power. Keep your humor power evergreen with timeless humor that flourishes like a fir tree.

DON'TS FOR DOING

As you apply your humor power to communicate, what you *don't* do can be effective.

1. *Don't Miss the Point—Hit Your Target*

Jokes that go astray fail to carry your message, may hit the wrong target, and damage your reputation as a humorist and communicator. And missing your target can be disastrous, as the following vignette shows.

"At an auto plant, an instructor told a novice, 'Look, I'm putting the rivet here in the right place. When I nod my head, hit it with the hammer.' She did. The instructor left a wife and four children."

Before you tell a joke, be certain you know it well and can put it across without missing the point. That's true of short humor, and it's essential for a longer story. Practice your story, especially when you're going to tell it to a group. Use mnemonic devices—if they work for you.

A man named Ralph had trouble remembering names. He tried the device of associating a name with a familiar object. At a party, he met, and liked, a woman named Hazel. A week later, he saw her at another party, but he couldn't think of her name.

"I do know you," Ralph insisted. "Your name is—oh, I remember. You're some kind of a nut."

Stories about missing a point can make points, with humor power. Billie Hurst, reference librarian at Southwest Missouri State University in Springfield, refers us to a real-life example. It happened several years ago to an office worker—call her Jane.

Basically, Jane disapproved of the off-color stories told by another woman at the office. Yet, being human, she wanted to prove she, too, could tell a funny story. When she heard a story that was apparently funny to some of her friends, she resolved to repeat it to her co-workers.

Here's the joke Jane heard.

A secretary started a new job, and the other employees warned her about their lecherous boss. "Stay away from the couch in his office," they advised.

The boss buzzed for the secretary. Notebook in hand, she entered his office and looked around cautiously. She checked every corner, but there was no couch.

And was she floored!

The joke Jane told was much the same—except for the last line.

"There wasn't any couch," said Jane, "and was she surprised!"

Mistold stories, cited as examples, make the point: communicate clearly. And Miss Hurst's story reminds us:

2. Don't Try the Offensive—Communicate Cleanly

Jane isn't the only person who objects to smutty stories. While the story she mistold was racy rather than ribald, it might offend some listeners. Yes, even in this "permissive age."

When Federal Judge Edmund Palmieri ruled on the importing of materials by the Kinsey Institute for Sex Research in 1958, he said, "Obscenity to one person is a subject of scientific inquiry to another." That works in reverse!

You know when it's all right to tell an off-color story to a friend, or to two or three persons. As the number of listeners grows—at a party, for example, or an office conference—the probability that off-color humor will be offensive to some increases.

Sexual jokes and jokes about bodily functions can cause discomfort among groups. You may provoke giggles and grins, but, chances are, you won't get your message across. Everyone will be too busy looking to see who else seems to be amused. Such humor can create problems for listeners who wonder, "Is my boss laughing?" "Is it okay for me to laugh?" "Did my son understand that?"

Sometimes, misunderstandings can lead to happy endings. Consider this story: A New Yorker in Las Vegas for a convention took his nine-year-old son to a show. It turned out that the topless girls were wearing a couple of patches of blue and gray. The nine-year-old reacted with, "Wow! Wow! This is great."

His father tried to figure how to handle it, but the boy continued excitedly, "They're wearing our school colors."

Most problems created by off-color humor can't be resolved this happily. If even one listener finds the humor offensive, communication is weakened throughout the group. That's why I aim for "all cleans, no dirties."

What is clean, and what is dirty? Opinions and reactions vary, but it's easier for a listener to read a dirty meaning into a joke than it is to communicate cleanly. *When in doubt* about a quip or story, *don't* use it.

HELP OTHERS REMEMBER YOUR MESSAGE

As a communications system, humor power can be applied to help us remember things. Children under six remember their "lollipops." Help others remember *your* message.

Personalize Your Humor Power

At the mammoth shopping mart, a little girl got lost. Her mother rushed to the manager to ask for help. Before any action could be taken, she heard her daughter calling, "Elaine! Elaine!"

Mother and daughter had a happy reunion. After she had hugged and kissed the child, Mother asked, "Why did you say 'Elaine'? Why didn't you say 'Mother'?"

"There are lots of mothers in this place," the little girl answered. "I wanted to be sure I got the right one."

Personalize your messages to Elaine, or Edwin, or both. Reach the right person, or persons, with the right approach. You and your messages will be more memorable!

Don't belittle others. If there's any hint of a put-down in a humor-power application, apply it to yourself—even if you have to fiddle with the facts a little. Make yourself the object of the jest, but . . .

Be good to yourself! You deserve consideration, too. Your self-directed kidding should be well removed from self-directed sarcasm. Give your humor power the personal touch, and try a little tenderness.

Be specific—about places, things, and, most of all, people. Telling a story about a man, tell it about a particular man. Or quote a friend as the source of your story. Don't say you were visiting a city. Make it Louisville or Denver or Oklahoma City. A listener's enjoyment increases in proportion to the extent he can identify with the situation and, up to a point, believe it.

In Annapolis

An Annapolis, Maryland, mother of three teen-agers solved the staying-out-late problem. She ruled that the last one in on Saturday night had to fix Sunday breakfast for the family.

—MARTIN A. RAGAWAY

Personalize that story. Give the Annapolis mother the name of someone you know. And change Annapolis to the name of your city or a nearby town. Or, to kid the residents of a big city or an entire region, quote a famous person. In this vignette substitute other big city names:

From Chicago

Mark Twain "quoted" Satan as saying to a newcomer, "The trouble with you Chicago people is that you think you are the best people down here, whereas you are merely the most numerous."

Texans, of course, are used to being kidded. Stories about them carry easy-to-remember messages of big ideas and generous notions. You might tell this one, saying that it happened to your friend Walt.

Walt did a favor for a Texan who insisted he wanted to give him something in return. Walt protested but finally said, "Well, maybe a few golf clubs." A day later, he received a telegram from the Texan. "Have six golf clubs for you, but only two have swimming pools."

In Minneapolis, it's told, they don't read the New Testament. Too much in it about St. Paul.

The first time a man goes to Vegas, he tries to win. All other times after that, he tries to get even.

In-flight dialogue: "What did the plane's captain say?"

"He said, 'We are approaching Las Vegas. Please fasten your money belts.'"

Be specific about persons and places, and you'll increase the validity of your humor power. In addition, use product names to make your message memorable:

TEACHER: Mike, what are the three great American parties?

MIKE: Democratic, Republican, and Tupperware.

TV commercials tell us something about ourselves. We have lemonade with imitation lemon juice—and Tidy Bowl and Pledge with real lemon juice.

He drinks. In fact, he deducts Johnny Walker as a dependent on his income tax.

Jack Nicklaus is going to do some Geritol commercials. For people who are under par?

They've invented a combination Polaroid camera and training bra—for girls who want to develop in sixty seconds.

Fictionalize Your Humor Power

"Have you heard the one about . . . ?" "That reminds me of a story." "Stop me if you've heard this one before."

In the telling of a joke, such beginnings may act as signals to stop listening. Who can remember an unheard message? Of course, there are special circumstances. A joke will always be funny, and be remembered, no matter how a purchasing agent tells it to a supplier!

In general, your story will put your message across more memorably when you tell it as an incident that happened to someone. Even if "someone" is "your wife's third cousin twice removed." Create the illusion of reality and enhance your validity—by fictionalizing fact.

I admit it. Not all of the stories I've told in this book happened the way I told them. Some of them didn't actually happen at all. But all of them have an element of actuality, in line with my belief that to win trust we have to be what we say we are and do what we say we're going to do. For example, in the area of humor about women:

The vignettes I tell about my wife and daughters may not be literally factual, but they're based on relatively real experiences and are not meant to be denigrating. And the actuality is that our most overlooked secret is the potential of women from the neck up—an opinion I've held and expressed throughout my career as a speaker.

Splendid!

Seldom any splendid story is entirely true.

—SAMUEL JOHNSON

Others will approve, and accept your most outrageous exaggerations, *if* you make them believable. Fiction reinforces fact.

Erma Bombeck, humorist and homemaker, has often written about her husband and their family of three young adults. As she presents it, this family of characters is more fictional than factual. In one of her earliest newspaper columns, she wrote about asking her husband to put up some Christmas lights. He changed the porch light from a forty-watt bulb to a sixty-watter. Or so she pretended, in a spirit of fun.

Art Fettig of Battle Creek, Michigan, humorist, author, and speaker, has this suggestion: "Blame it on the younger generation." Art's idea is that when an individual wants to put together a string of jokes, he will be more believable—and less likely to be thought of as a bore or a smart aleck—"if he lays the blame on his daughter, for instance. Blame it on the younger generation! These kids are marvelous."

In this area, Art has paid his dues, for his book *It Only Hurts When I Frown* is based on the humor power in family life.

"I told my daughter Nancy that I would spend the day with winners, and just for contrast, I wanted some loser jokes," Art says, spreading the blame. "I asked her to go over to the college and tell those kids I would pay ten bucks for the best loser jokes they came up with. Listen to this one. 'A loser is a guy who gets a kidney transplant from a bed wetter.'

"Have you seen some of the bumper stickers that are going around? I laugh, and then I forget them, so I had my son Dan make a hobby of collecting the ones he liked most. Some are wild. 'McDonalds has small buns.' "

Those collections suggest another way we can make our messages clearer and easier to remember.

Use Familiar Vehicles for Your Humor Power

"For all you science buffs: Does the name Pavlov ring a bell?"

We're conditioned to smile or laugh at familiar forms of humor. Drive your messages home with humor power in a currently popular "vehicle." For example, I like to make points with *loser jokes*.

He's not very bright. Bought the exclusive rights to sell maps of movie stars' homes in downtown Des Moines, Iowa.

He's not very bright. His wife bought him an electric blanket, and he tried to play it.

He's a loser. At 9:15 A.M., he asked the boss for a raise. At 9:16 A.M., he asked for a reference.

A loser is a man who pays a thousand dollars for a cemetery lot, then drowns at sea.

A fat loser is one who doesn't. He stretched out at the beach, and a kid painted "Goodyear" on his belly. He went to the zoo, and the kids fed him peanuts. So he called for an ambulance and got a crane.

Another vehicle, the "crossing" joke, seems to be particularly popular with the younger generation.

A scientist crossed an intersection with a new car and got a blonde. A farmer crossed a hen with a banjo and got a chicken that plucks itself. My neighbor crossed a swordfish with a giraffe and got a great tree surgeon. And a furrier who does his own breeding crossed a mink with a gorilla. He got a great coat, but the sleeves were too long.

"Show me, and I'll show you" jokes are currently popular,

but like most vehicles for humor, they have a long history. "Show me a liar, and I'll show thee a thief," wrote George Herbert, clergyman, poet, and creator of aphorisms, back in 1651.

Today's versions include: Show me a man who walks with his head held high, and I'll show you a man who hasn't got used to his bifocals. Show me a man who has kissed the Blarney Stone, and I'll show you a man with a sex problem. And, from the world of sports, show me a good loser, and I'll show you a real loser.

"Good news–bad news" jokes carry messages with humor power.

A senior citizen told me that, after you hit seventy, there's good news and bad news. The good news is, you've still got lust in your heart. The bad news is, you have rust everywhere else.

Good news! A survey shows college girls are most attracted to middle-aged men. Bad news! They think middle-aged means thirty-two.

A psychiatrist told a patient the good news. "You don't have an inferiority complex." Then came the bad news. "You *are* inferior."

"Good news and bad," a wife told her husband. "The good news is that all those premiums you've been paying through the years for auto insurance aren't going to be wasted."

Many messages can be powered by the familiar humor of how small, tough, or poor your hometown was. If you do tell a joke about a small town, affirm your reliability. Establish the fact, or the fictionalized fact, that you come from a small town.

My hometown was so small that, at the four-way stop, only two of the ways went anywhere. My hometown was so small that when you opened the back door you were out of town.

My hometown was very tough. If you weren't home by 9 P.M., the cops declared you legally dead. In my hometown, folks were so poor we thought "day-old bread" was a brand name.

The same format can be used to make points when kidding your friends and associates.

When I was in the Marines, we had a drill sergeant who was so tough he used to wear a wig. What's so tough about that? He kept it on with a nail.

Our football coach was so tough he had to take showers. What's so tough about that? He couldn't take a bath because when he did, the waters would part.

Let me tell you how smart my lawyer is. He never graduated from law school. What's so smart about that? He was so smart he settled out of class.

Messages travel far on bumper stickers.

On a mail truck in Alexandria, Virginia: Old mailmen never die. They just lose their zip.

On a compact car in Albuquerque, New Mexico: I am neither for, nor against, apathy.

On a Brownsville, Texas, car: We support mental health like crazy.

Dr. Charles W. Jarvis, a speaker, writer, and humorist based in San Marcos, Texas, shared this one with me. "I saw an interesting bumper sticker the other day," he told me. "It said, 'Bumper Sticker.'"

Definitions put humor power to work in a familiar way.

Coo-munication: A baby puts a message across.

Automatic: You can't repair it yourself.

Virus: Latin, defined by doctors as "Your guess is as good as mine."

The expanded definition reflects your perspective and is related to the metaphor.

On a bus, it's called "congestion." In a night club, it's called "intimacy."

"Security" once meant having enough money to last you the rest of your life. Now it means having enough to last the rest of the month.

The best way to live happily ever after is not to be after too much.

Spring in Indiana is when the furnace clicks off and the sump pump goes on.

Creative selling is the lumber dealer who calls you up in

the middle of the night and, in a deep voice, tells you to build an ark.

If your message is "Have fun," try some wacky definitions.

Attest: An examination.

Attire: Goes around wheels.

Murals: Rules of good behavior.

Diffuse: The string on the end of a firecracker.

Custom: Don't we all?

Familiar forms of humor help you make a point, quickly and directly. You can take a short cut around involved explanations, saving words and time. For humor power, content as well as form should be easy to recognize.

This, too, is a kind of conditioning. After twenty-five years of speaking and creating humor power in all sorts of situations, I'm convinced that conditioning is highly important in, and perhaps essential to, effective use of this power.

Suppose you have a message for a group, and you want to humanize yourself—by letting your listeners know you have problems with your golf game. You might say, "Have you golfers out there found that by the time you can afford to lose a golf ball, you can't hit it that far?"

That's effective—as long as most of your listeners are golfers. Non-golfers rarely appreciate the point, and why should they? They haven't been conditioned to do so. "I lost four balls, three in the ball washer" makes a point to a golfer. To non-golfers, it has all the meaning of a foreign language they don't want to know.

It's the same for tennis and non-tennis players. You can tell a tennis buff, "You have something to be proud of. Your game is older than golf. Tennis is mentioned in the Bible. It says Moses served in Pharaoh's court." But don't serve too many tennis jokes to a group.

Humor power saves explanations only when we don't have to explain it! Arthur Secord, a speaker, writer, and recording artist based in Sun City Center, Florida, uses a classic example about a rider who said to a hunter: "You can have your deer, but first let me remove my saddle."

"There is no humor," Art Secord points out, "if we have to answer the question, 'How did he get a saddle on a deer?'"

Individuals who haven't been conditioned to think funny about golf will, of course, find some relaxing enjoyment in such dialogues as: "I'm wearing my golf socks today." "What golf socks?" "The ones with eighteen holes in them." But they will reach the boredom point more quickly than the avid golfer. Tell not just a few but a lot of golf jokes, and the avid golfer will get there, too!

That's the case with any subject. Watch the proportions of your humor power. Too many items in one area can tangle the wires of communication and short-circuit your message. Vary the proportions! Vary them, especially, in daily life, when you hope to put a message across to one or two persons. You'll be most convincing, and most memorable, to those who know you best and see you most often, if you can make a point with a variety of humor-powered examples.

Easy-to-recognize humor in familiar forms does have a drawback. Popular jokes travel around until everyone knows them, and they exhaust their point-making potential, at least temporarily. Stash many-told tales in your humor-power reservoir, and bring them out later, refreshed. They will supply you with resources when you need a point-maker for a specific idea.

Give a well-traveled joke, or your own funny thoughts, a twist, and look at the familiar in a new way. When you can see the funny side of almost any situation, creating humor power with a sudden twist follows naturally.

Consider an ordinary situation. A nervous passenger on an elevator might ask the operator, "What would happen if a cable broke? Would we go up or down?" The operator might reply, "That depends on the kind of life you've led."

MOTIVATE!
MAKE OTHERS EAGER TO ACT

The student asked, "It says here that if we study hard, don't drink, don't smoke, and don't run around with girls, we'll live longer. Is that true?"

The professor answered, "We won't know for sure until someone tries it."

Getting others to try your idea, suggestion, or strategy is the important third step in putting your message across with a boost from humor power. The first two—communicating clearly and helping others remember—help you motivate.

"I'm collecting," said the newspaper carrier. "Fine," said the customer. "Your money is over there in the bushes, where I usually find my newspaper."

Adjust your aim, and focus your humor power to be a memorable communicator. Sometimes individuals may miss your message because they don't fully realize it's meant for them. Let a story about Johnny's misunderstanding help you say to others, "This message is for you!"

"I don't want to scare anybody," said Johnny to his teacher, "but my dad says if my report card doesn't get better, somebody's going to get a spanking."

Appeal to the interests of an individual or group. Win interest, and you win co-operation. Another story suggests that we can't communicate and co-operate until we can meet on the common ground of shared interests and clear motives.

At the movies, a romantically minded couple found the theater crowded. She had to sit in one row, while he sat in the row ahead of her. The young woman thought she could solve the problem by asking the man next to her to change seats with her young man.

"Excuse me," she whispered. "Are you alone?"

The man in the next seat didn't answer, and she repeated her question. Silently, he stared ahead. She tried again, louder.

"Cut it out!" he told her. "My wife and kids are here."

Condition others to receive your message with humor-powered examples. Inspire them with eagerness to act. This example helps you show creativity at work in motivation:

When a little boy arrived home with an ice-cream cone in each hand, his mother asked, "Did you spend all your money?"

"Didn't spend anything," the boy answered.

"Someone treated you," Mother guessed.

The little boy shook his head.

"You didn't steal them?"

"No."

"Then how did you get those ice-cream cones?"

"I told the girl at the counter to put a chocolate cone in one hand and a peppermint cone in the other. Then I told her she could reach in my pocket for the money, but please be careful not to bother my pet snake."

Condition yourself to see humor power in terms of the needs and wishes of others. Begin by appreciating *their* humor power. You'll develop the ability to motivate as you discover more about the "why" of others' smiles and laughter.

Why Laugh?

She laughs at everything you say. Why? Because she has fine teeth.

—BENJAMIN FRANKLIN

Help your humor power grow by receiving others' messages with a willingness to be amused. When our associates express themselves humorously, we have an obligation to respond smilingly—and not with the put-down of a frozen face.

Alert: If we want to motivate an individual in a personal or business situation, we may offend if we smile too much, at every mildly humorous remark he makes. We're certain to offend if we automatically assume our humor power is stronger, keener, and quicker than his.

Don't!

If you wish to lower yourself in a person's favor, one good way is to tell his story over again, the way *you* heard it.

—MARK TWAIN

When we repeatedly top others' jokes, that may be humor, but it isn't humor power. Speaker and humorist Ray Stanish, Albuquerque, shares an example from personal experience.

"Many years ago, I worked for a boss who liked to tell jokes," Ray says. "He wasn't all that funny, but he wasn't bad. Still, I could usually top his story—and I did."

Ray doesn't recall a specific joke he topped. Suppose we take an earlier example.

BOSS: I wish cheap clothes looked good on me.

RAY: They do.

"After several of my toppings," Ray continues, "he said, 'Can't you let me have just one?' There's a case where my humor, poorly applied, resulted in my losing power instead of gaining it. I've always remembered that experience. I learned from it."

We gain when we: Remember that it's better if we don't always top another's joke; appreciate and motivate; send messages along the two-way channel of humor power.

Shake Hands!

"Cavemen shook hands to show they had no weapons to harm each other," says Marty Ragaway, editor of the humor service *Funny, Funny World*. "Greeting another person with humor is saying, in effect, 'I am not going to harm you. I'm able to laugh at myself, and I'm sharing with you something we can both enjoy.'"

Humor power is an improvement on the handshake. Show and share it. Put your message across, to one individual, or to many.

8 Humor Power When You're on Your Feet

Everyone makes a speech sometime or the other, somewhere or the other—at a luncheon or banquet, at church, school, PTA, service or social club meeting, on the job, or elsewhere in daily life. Even though you don't think of yourself as a speaker, a look back will remind you that you have given speeches. A look ahead will show more speechmaking to come.

As your humor power grows, you'll find yourself called on to "say a few words" more and more often. Nervous? Don't be. Just have a good opening and a good closing, and keep the two as close together as possible! That isn't, of course, as simple as it sounds, but there's a lot of truth in it. To make a speech immortal, you don't have to make it everlasting.

At a convention once, I heard a delegate compliment the previous speaker. "You were much better than our last speaker," the delegate said. "He talked for an hour and never said anything. You took only fifteen minutes."

It's much easier for a speaker to talk a lot than it is for him to say anything. But making a speech isn't hard work—unless you would honestly rather be doing something else.

I want to share with you some of the things I've learned about humor power in speaking during twenty-five years on the platform. You might call it a twenty-five-year research project, since I'm still studying and learning. I'm fortunate in being able to share, too, some ideas and suggestions from other speakers. All are accomplished professionals, noted for their presentations. Their understanding and comments have been helpful to me, and I'm confident their stories of platform experiences will be helpful to you. You've met some of these speakers in earlier chapters. You'll meet more in this chapter.

Whether you speak in public often or just once in a while, what we share here can enable you to put humor power to work, not only in speaking but in daily life. Long before you're on the platform, your speech begins with planning, preparation, and practice. For the present, let's start where you come on.

"INTRODUCING THE GREAT MR. UH . . ."

The second most difficult thing a speaker has to learn, it's been said, is not to nod when the introducer is praising him.

How to get the right introduction may not be the *most* difficult, but it's close. Write your own introduction, or have someone write it for you. Get it to the toastmaster, emcee, or other introducer ahead of time.

Otherwise, you may be presented as the great "Uh," and be all tangled up with jokes, comments, and announcements that the introducer felt he had to make.

Alert: If your name is unusual and/or difficult to pronounce, help your introducer put it across with humor power. Or, do it yourself. Let your audience know you've had name problems, with a think-funny illustration:

"What's your name?" "Tex." "Oh, you're from Texas." "No, Louisiana." "Then why do you call yourself Tex?" "Well, I'd rather be called Tex than Louise."

Here are a couple of examples from real life. When speaker Ray Monsalvatge said his name, he explained, "Monsalvatge rhymes with itchy-scratchy." Speaker Tom Haggai of High Point, North Carolina, tells his audiences, "It's an advantage to have a name as odd as this, although I haven't figured out what that advantage is as yet."

Keep your written introduction brief and clear. Help the introducer look good, and establish your own validity and reliability. Introducers, especially the most talented and skilled ones, will appreciate the time you save them by providing a written introduction. The better they are, the busier they're likely to be—and the more delighted to get a lift from your work and time. This supposes, of course, that we don't approach our introducer in the spirit of "Look, you jerk, I know you're going to goof this up, so I wrote what *I* want you to say."

Establish a good relationship with your introducer. That's important, too. Witness what happened to a politician scheduled to speak at a dinner for sportswriters. Arthur "Bugs" Baer, sportswriter and humorist, had a poor opinion of the politician, but he agreed to introduce him. "I have been asked," Bugs began, "to introduce a man who is respected for his integrity, loved for his humanitarianism, and admired for his courage."

He continued, in the same vein, closing with "a leader, an individual of vision, a brilliant co-ordinator, a superb administrator." And then he paused. "I have been asked to introduce such a man," he said, "but I don't think he's here tonight."

Then Bugs Baer sat down!

"Be there," in the good opinion of your introducer. Prepare the most effective introduction you can, and let your introducer take all the credit. That will win, for both of you. When Thelma Howard, my program manager, sends out a copy of my introduction, she includes a note, "Avoid saying Herb wrote or provided you with this intro, 'cause he didn't—I did!"

In spite of careful preparation, your introduction may not turn out exactly the way you planned. React with humor power! Speaker Dave Yoho of Fairfax, Viriginia, shares a memory of an introduction that failed. "I had to get the audience back with me," he explained, "so I said, 'I wish I could say that was the greatest introduction I ever had, but it isn't.'"

Dave continued, "When good old Charlie here asked me about what to say in the introduction, I suggested, 'Why not play down the fact that I'm attractive and brilliant, and say something about my humility?'

"The greatest introduction I ever had was at the Home Builders Convention in Houston. It's the biggest convention of its kind in the world—about fifty-three thousand people there, and they were going to hear *me?* I wanted a great introduction. And I got one.

"I gave it myself."

Dr. Kenneth McFarland of Topeka, Kansas, speaker, author, and recording artist, suggests another way to handle an introduction that falls flat. Kid yourself—as he did:

"You know how it is on the last day of a convention," Ken said. "They thank all the local committees and tell the delegates, 'It's all over, boys.' *Then* they say, 'Now, here's McFarland.' I feel like the man who was driving the wrong way on a one-way street. 'I must be late; everybody's going home.'"

An overly enthusiastic introduction can pose a problem, too. Again, Ken McFarland kidded himself: "He sold me! I am convinced that you actually are fortunate to have me here."

As you develop your own ways of responding to the introduction and helping yourself and the audience to settle down, you can build on ideas that others have used.

"I feel like the bear who fell into the honey barrel. I hope my tongue is equal to the challenge."

"I've practiced this speech all week, and I feel pretty good about it. So, if you can just manage to look a little more like a bathroom mirror, we'll get on with it."

Two Things

"There are only two things more difficult than making after-dinner speeches," said Winston Churchill. "One is climbing a wall leaning toward you, and the other is kissing a girl leaning away from you."

If you're nervous, admit it, get the audience with you, and calm down by saying something like, "Your chairman told me not to be a loser. He said a loser is a speaker who took *two* aspirin, and the butterflies started playing 'ping' with *one* of them."

Reacting quickly to the introduction calls for thinking funny and quipping on your feet—an ability you'll need throughout your speech.

"AD-LIB"
Your Humor Power

To "ad-lib," says the dictionary, is to improvise or speak spontaneously. But the way a one-liner tells it, "An ad-libber is a guy who stays up all night to memorize spontaneous jokes." The fact is, many of the ad libs you and I hear and use are the result of planning and preparation. Humor power lies not so much in spontaneity as in making quips *sound* spontaneous.

Benjamin Disraeli, British prime minister, was congratulated by a young woman. "That was a wonderful impromptu speech you gave!"

"My dear," said Disraeli, "I have been preparing that impromptu speech for twenty years."

Plan and prepare your "impromptu" stories, your "improvised" quips.

Do It Yourself

"I am not going to pray for you," said Archbishop Fulton J. Sheen. "There are certain things a man has to do for himself. He has to blow his own nose, make his own love, and say his own prayers."

Creating ad libs is something you must do for yourself, too. Work on your humor power and use it, not just now and then or just when you're speaking, but whenever a good opportunity offers. Work hard. Soon, point-making thoughts, quips, and vignettes will spring to mind naturally, and you will indeed be able to display spontaneous wit, winning respect in speaking and in daily living.

Great ad-libbers get that way by working at it until quipping on their feet comes naturally. Comedian/actor Frank Fay was famous as an ad-libber in difficult situations. During one of his night-club acts, a listener heckled him and, finally, shouted, "Aw, you stink!"

"Have a care, sir," Frank Fay replied, "you are speaking of the man I love."

When quips occur to us spontaneously, they're often worth saving and repeating. That noteworthy ad-libber W. C. Fields was appearing in a production of the *Ziegfeld Follies*. During one performance, the scenery fell with a crash.

Exclaimed Fields, "Mice!"

The audience laughed so heartily that the scenery crash and Fields' ad lib were repeated in every performance of the show.

Let your audience help you sound spontaneous.

KNOW YOUR AUDIENCE

Before you speak, try to mingle with members of your audience, so you can put their humor power to work. Brief conversations can cue you in to their thoughts, their interests, their recent activities. You'll gather material for "impromptu" anecdotes and quips that will personalize your speech and make it more timely, more appropriate.

You can fictionalize a little, too. For mixed audiences, speaker/writer Art Fettig likes this one.

"I met a friend in the lobby, and I said to her, 'Loretta, you're wearing your wedding ring on the wrong finger.'

" 'Well,' Loretta answered, 'I married the wrong man.' "

George Bailey of Freeport, Pennsylvania, memory expert and entertainer, gets acquainted with his audience in advance in a unique manner. As part of his program, he greets up to one hundred guests before the meeting. When it's over, he pays five dollars to anyone whose name he forgets.

That approach resulted in a bonus—a humor-powered example that is still working for him. George Bailey tells the story.

"During one performance about twenty years ago, a noisy character in the front row was giving me a bit of trouble—not serious, but irksome. I had just finished calling off the names of one hundred people in the audience.

"This fellow in the front row didn't wait until I had begun an explanation of my method of remembering names and faces. He just up and loudly asked, 'Mishter Bailey, how do you remember all those names?'

"Aiming to quiet him down, I replied, 'Sir, I can tell you in three words. It takes brains.'

"Without one extra burp he came back with, 'Thash what *I* thought. What do *you* use?'

"After that rebuttal, this memory expert was completely put down, and the crowd roared louder than at anything else that happened that night. What a good show it turned out to be!

"I've used that story—and it's a true one—many, many times since, and it still gets a good response," George Bailey tells us. "Yes, the use of humor power has helped to spruce up my explanation of how to remember names and faces."

The better you know your listeners, their circumstances, and their mood, the more effectively you'll be able to identify with them in a relevant and timely manner. Joe Powell of Alexandria, Virginia, speaker, filmwright, and author, illustrates that point with a personal, and humor-powered, example. He told the following story in his book *Executive Speaking —An Acquired Skill*.

Joe was scheduled to be the keynote speaker at an insurance company president's early-bird breakfast—seven o'clock on a Sunday morning! The president was supercharged with energy. He had started his meeting the night before with a convivial dinner dance that lasted till 3 A.M. For him, four hours of sleep was more than enough. He wanted to see if his sales force could measure up to his stamina.

Unfortunately, the hotel's hot-water system broke down during the night. Came the dawn, and the hungover survivors of the night before prepared to shave, hot-shower, and simulate alertness for their command attendance at the breakfast. Then they discovered there was no hot water for shaving or showering. At breakfast, they discovered there would be no coffee, tea, or other beverage needing hot water. The audience confronting Joe Powell was, he says, "disgruntled, unhappy, uncomfortable—and damn mad."

Capitalizing on his knowledge of the circumstances and the mood, Joe made this seemingly innocent opening remark: "This is the first time I have seen an insurance company president have an opening Saturday-night brawl, and not even one person got into *hot water.*"

Audience frustration dissolved. Everyone laughed at himself and at the absurdity of the situation. Keyed to that situation, the humor power of a simple play on words triggered and released pent-up emotion—and created a responsive audience.

Put yourself in Joe Powell's place. At least, put yourself on the platform. You've been introduced. What now? Your quick reaction to your introduction will lead into your opening. In fact, it may *be* your opening.

OPEN—and OPEN UP
—with Humor Power

You're on. Now, all you have to do is get the full attention of the audience. Next, keep that attention throughout your speech —even though attention flits like a hummingbird.

Tough? It can be done. Sam Hunter of Sun City, Arizona, has been getting and holding audience attention for nearly forty years. Sam does it, he tells us, by "using humor for power." His humor power creates high drama in a fictitious situation made to look real. It grabs the audience.

"I'm an imposter, acting as a visitor sitting in the audi-

ence," Sam explains. "The emcee singles me out for some outrageous reason and asks me, suddenly, to pinch-hit for the
main speaker, who is running late. I'm surprised, shocked, and
scared. I make them believe I'm in trouble. I say words back-
ward and stutter.

"The audience is shocked, surprised. The situation is very
emotional, but funny. My listeners feel sorry for me and almost angry at the emcee for putting me on the spot. Yet, it is
so funny, they give me one hundred per cent from then on—
when I keep my humor power going and use it to further a
point."

Sam Hunter, known as "Stuttering Sam," is a genius at
juggling words—and a believer in humor power. He gains audience attention and empathy in a highly individual way.

As an occasional speaker, you may not want to invest time
in polishing the talents needed for a specialty act, such as
Sam's stuttering routine. But if you've already developed your
talent, for anything from juggling to singing, by all means use
it in your speaking. Use it as a potent force to create respect
and to assure a warmer welcome for your humor power and
your message.

Your opening offers two options. You can take the rapid-
fire approach of the instant attention-getter. Or you can try a
slower buildup, taking a few minutes—a very few—to let your
listeners know what you plan to share with them.

Either way, humor power can help you move smoothly to
the substance of your speech. Suppose you want to discuss
some of the problems of teaching and learning. You could tell
this vignette.

A Texas youngster rushed up to his mother and told her
he needed holsters, pistol, and gun belt for kindergarten.
Mother asked why, and the youngster said, " 'Cause the
teacher is going to teach us to draw."

Or, you might turn to this thought: "To earn more, learn
more." Then explain. A man entered a jackass in the Kentucky
Derby. He didn't expect him to win, but he thought the association might do him good.

When you plan to talk about "We don't know what we can do till we try," try this one.

A golfer told his partner, "I'm anxious to make this shot. That's my mother-in-law on the clubhouse porch."

The partner replied, "Don't be a fool. It's two hundred yards. You can't hit her from here."

A humor-powered opening is your opportunity to set up a winning relationship with your listeners, one that you can sustain throughout the speech.

John Wolfe of Houston, lecturer, author, and motivational-film star, says, "As I see it, one of the important objectives of humor power is to get the audience to like the speaker as well as the speech. If they like the guy who's talking, they have to like what he says!"

That's why John makes points by laughing at himself. In discussing the importance of time, one of his favorites is, "I still remember back in World War II, they gave us these little pills to stop us thinking about girls. I'm finding out now, they're just beginning to work!"

Again, when time is the subject, John Wolfe finds this one always goes over, especially with a mixed audience.

"People tell me I'm in pretty good shape for a fellow my age, and I owe it all to my wife, Alice. When we got married twenty-five years ago, I told her, 'Honey, you and I will never have an argument. Any time you bug me about something, I won't argue. I'll just take a walk around the block.'

"So this magnificent physique you see here—it's just a quarter of a century of outdoor living!"

Turn your humor power on yourself. Make your point, and create that winning relationship. After an introducer kids me about our large family, mentioning that Betty Ann and I have eight children, I may respond by involving my audience.

"Anybody in the audience who has a large family?" I ask.

And an answer comes back, "Yes, we also have eight."

"Great! Which mental institution is your wife in?"

Or I might say, "Can I ask you a question, sir? Do you ever get the feeling you are developing the kind of kids you don't want yours to play with?"

The introduction and my reaction condition the audience to get ready for a speaker who takes himself lightly, and his job seriously. Condition *your* audience.

SHOW YOUR AUDIENCE
Your Humor Power

One theory holds that humor in its highest form is visual, not verbal. I believe people don't laugh at words, they laugh at themselves. Sometimes using a visual aid helps to show them it's all right to laugh. Of course, the poor soul who *listens* to something that amuses others and then says, "I don't see anything funny about that," can't *see* the point, either.

Pretty Funny

Two men saw the great pantomimist, Marcel Marceau, perform.

"You know," one said to the other, "that guy would be pretty funny, if he could only talk."

Over the years, I've used "sight laughs" from visual aids to get results. When D. H. Lawrence's novel *Lady Chatterly's Lover* came out, I had a book that I could open up and the book would begin to burn. Today, there are a lot of books you could mention if you wanted to try that idea.

Another time, I used to say, "I want to make these seven points," and I'd hold up my hand to show seven fingers. False fingers, naturally—at least two! In addition, to dramatize the idea of persistence, I had a candle that wouldn't go out.

With sight jokes, you gain extra dividends in audience response. *Show* something that ties in with a humor-powered point.

"Ladies and gentlemen, a few nights ago I was in Chicago. I had the pleasure of addressing the Executives' Club at Hotel —now, what was the name of that hotel? Just a moment, I have it right here."

Reach inside your coat pocket, pull out a silver spoon, and "read" it. "It was the Hilton hotel." Or the Regency, or the Marriott.

Alert: When you combine sight and sound in a joke, try to use something which is unexpected as well as clever. Be sure every person in the audience can see the gimmick you use!

Gimmicks lighten the moment and get results. On another level, I apply humor power in the form of multicolored slides. Ninety per cent of my presentations are illustrated by multigraphics. They help me to be an "Edu-Tainer."

Most of the slides are custom-created, not only to fit my subjects but, importantly, to serve the needs and goals of my clients. In a TEAM effort, we begin by learning what a group wants to have happen as a result of my presentation. Then the slides are designed and developed for that goal. Since they are custom jobs, it's impossible to give you a "typical" example, but here are a couple of general examples.

On the screen, a large, colorful image appears. Arching across the gleeful cartoon figure of a gas pump, a rainbow reaches a pot of gold. Lettering proclaims that the pump is "full up" with "wonder fuel."

The wonder fuel is enthusiasm, a powerful propellant and one of my favorite topics. It lifts an individual above the commonplace. It provides a vital spark. If *you* have it, it will help you immensely in creating your humor power.

Another full-color slide shows what is, all too often, "the life cycle of an idea," with a vertical row illustrating five light bulbs that go from bright to dim to dark. Turning off the light of an idea are these lettered reactions: "It can't be done"; "It won't work"; "It's too expensive"; "It won't last"; and "I knew it all the time."

Sound familiar? You've heard those before, I know. They're no joke.

Even without slides, you can make your humor power visual in simple but effective ways. For example, attach a comic book to a chart and mount the chart on a wall. Even simpler, grab a comic book and hold it aloft.

What are you going to say about the comic book? One

line that goes with it is, "Now science is only fifty years behind the comic books." When you put your own feelings into this one-liner, the message you reinforce could be "We expect too much from science or technology," or its opposite, "We need to expand the scope of our scientific goals."

A teacher at a Midwestern university offers another example of effective visual humor, so simple it didn't even need an extra prop.

Ralph Nader was in town for an evening meeting at the university. He wasn't going to speak about consumer problems. He wasn't going to speak. In fact, he wasn't even going to sit on the platform. But just the idea that he would be present set the campus buzzing.

Before the main program, a popular local pianist was to set the mood by playing a few notes. He walked across the stage and sat down on the piano stool. Then, slowly and carefully, he adjusted and buckled an imaginary seat belt!

Remember, you're visible! Be your own best visual aid. Simple gestures, keyed to words, can create visual humor. Here's something I've used:

"He's an atheist. He wouldn't even cross the street."

As I say that, I make the sign of the Cross.

Alert: Don't overgesture! Except in a few rare cases, speakers who exaggerate their body motions soon have the audience watching their movements instead of hearing their message.

A youngster, making his first speech at school, asked his friends to watch, listen, and criticize him. After the speech, one young critic said, "I liked the way you talked, but I didn't like your gestures."

"Gestures?" said the speechmaker. "I had hives!"

Gestures and other body motions can be misunderstood.

One kind of motion, however, *can* help you communicate your humor power. Spoken humor often stumbles over the blocks of "he said, she said." *Move your head from one side to the other, to indicate a change of characters.* Get rid of "he said, she said"! For example:

"How did you spend that much money on groceries in one week?"

"Turn sideways and look in the mirror."

No trouble knowing who's who there! Here's another, on the liberation theme:

"Do you know a way to save a male chauvinist pig from drowning?"

"No!"

"Good!"

Along with moving your head, a name or title helps to distinguish one story character from another.

"I'm temporarily broke, *Doctor,* but I'll remember you in my will."

"That's all right. Oh, say, would you let me have the prescription blank back for a minute? There's one small change I want to make."

Here's a visual effect which has worked for some speakers. You might want to borrow and adapt it to your opening.

"Before I begin, I'd like to take a moment to recognize a few people in the audience."

Shade your eyes, look slowly around the room—and now and then let your face light up as you wave at someone.

Now for the simplest, most effective visual humor of all.

Use your smile. If you're not using your smile, in your speaking and in your life, you're like a person with a million dollars in the bank—and no checkbook.

KEEP YOUR AUDIENCE
with Humor Power

With humor power as part of your opening, you capture attention, create a mood, release tension when necessary, and establish rapport with your listeners. As you move into the substance of your speech, you will need to keep on doing more of what you've been doing.

The human attention span is short, especially when a

speaker drones on and on about one aspect of one subject. Of such speakers it has been said, "After his speech, there was a great awakening."

Excuse Him

In the midst of what seemed to be an everlasting speech, a man in the audience rose and left the room.

His wife hopped to her feet. "Please excuse my husband," she said. "He walks in his sleep."

Even the speaker laughed.

Recapture attention! Change the subject, or your approach to the subject. Give your audience the humor-power shock treatment with a quick one-liner.

Suppose you're speaking on a seasonal topic. You might say, "It's a fact that when there is a full moon people act differently. The crime rate goes up. That's reasonable. It's easier for muggers to see."

Give the same thought a twist, and a different setting, to bring back your listeners when you're talking about some aspect of human relations. "There isn't enough love in the world today. When you see two people with their arms around each other, chances are, one of them is a mugger."

Like the mugger, you're trying to raise funds for a cause. In your speech, adapt what the minister told his congregation. "I said often in my sermons that the poor are welcome in my church. By the size of the collection the past few Sundays, it looks like they finally came."

Keep your audience listening. Brief humor can give you the power to do this.

The topic is salesmanship, and you can say, perhaps about some humor-powered listener, "He's a good salesman. He finally got that receptionist to say yes. He asked her if she was busy tonight."

Again, it helps to be specific. To an audience interested in real estate, repeat the suburban prayer, "O Lord, please don't let the tax assessor find out what our neighbor sold his house for."

If we tell a joke just because it's funny, audience attention is likely to take off on one of those hummingbird flights. Don't drag humor in by the heels. *Make it relevant, make it part of your message, and make it humor power!*

When your subject is motivation, a story like this can be woven into your speech.

Hired as production manager at a manufacturing plant, Jack introduced several new ideas which increased production. Output went up thirty per cent in his first three months. Jack had other ideas, and production increased another ten per cent in the next few months.

The boss was pleased. He slapped Jack on the back and said, "You're doing a great job. Keep up the good work."

"Fine," said Jack, "but why don't you put that on my paycheck?"

"Done," said the boss. He kept his word.

When Jack got his next paycheck, he found this written across the bottom: "You're doing a great job. Keep up the good work."

If communications problems are your topic, let this story reinforce your message.

Gary called a doctor in the middle of the night. "Come quick! My wife is very sick. I think she has appendicitis."

"Gary, you're crazy," the doctor answered. "I took out your wife's appendix myself, six or seven years ago. Did you ever hear of a woman having a second appendix?"

"No," said Gary, "but didn't you ever hear of a man having a second wife?"

For religious messages, amusing examples have relevance.

When a salesman left his car in a no-parking zone, he also left a note. "I've circled this block twenty times. I have an appointment and must keep it or lose my job. Forgive us our trespasses." Returning, the salesman found a ticket with this note: "I've circled this block twenty years. If I don't give you a ticket, I'll lose my job. Lead us not into temptation."

Your platform may be a political stump. Whether you're

speaking at your local political club or campaigning for office, make humor power part of your message.

Three young fellows saved a politician from drowning. Gratefully, he asked what he could do to reward them.

FIRST: I'd like to go to West Point, but my grades are bad.

POLITICIAN: No problem. You're in.

SECOND: I was turned down at Annapolis.

POLITICIAN: Don't worry. You're in.

THIRD: I want to be buried in Arlington Cemetery.

POLITICIAN: Cemetery? How come?

THIRD: When my father hears I helped save you, he's going to kill me.

Those of you who speak at PTA meetings or address some other groups including parents might fit this story into your speech.

A fortyish matron was upset to learn she was pregnant.

Her doctor reassured her, "You're in good physical condition. You should have no trouble."

"I'm not worried about that," the matron said. "I just don't think I can stand twelve more years of PTA."

In your speaking as in your life, humor power can help you handle troublesome topics and situations. It works for you when your message is one people don't want to hear, whether the message deals with a painful reality, demands big sacrifices on their part, or asks them to face up to personal, community, and/or other problems. It gives you the power to set your listeners free from emotional pain and to ease tensions about taboo subjects.

In fact, some subjects are so serious they can best be handled with the gentle touch of humor power. For example, if your speech aims to raise funds for hospital expansion or equipment, you may need to deal with once-taboo subjects such as fatal illness or death. Of course, you'll avoid harsh humor. But you could lighten emotional pain for your listeners by telling a familiar anecdote about Henry David Thoreau.

At Thoreau's deathbed an aunt asked him, "Have you made your peace with God?"

Thoreau replied, "I didn't know we had quarreled."

Handle trouble with humor power. Use this power to create an attitude and an environment where listeners will let down their inhibitions and mellow their mood.

A fellow told a doctor on the phone, "My wife has just dislocated her jaw. If you're out this way this week or the week after, you might drop in."

Then there's the first-grade teacher who sent her morning attendance report to the principal marked, "Help! They are all here."

With humor power, establish your credentials to speak on troublesome topics. As you talk about any worthwhile subject, you will arouse feelings toward a person, an idea, or an institution. Take care not to stir up emotions that are too strong or too deep. Avoid making quips on subjects people feel too intensely about.

Your basic credentials consist of laughing at yourself. Great humorists have made us laugh by playfully acting out *our* baser impulses—as *their* impulses. They revealed things we cover or control and showed us the power in being able to laugh at them.

That Old Curmudgeon

Oscar Levant, pianist, actor, and humorist, chose "crusty curmudgeon" as his personal role.

"I don't have any enemies," he declared, "but all my friends hate me."

"I don't drink," he revealed. "I don't like liquor. It makes me feel good."

How far you want to go, in the direction of laughing at yourself by acting out non-noble impulses, depends on your

personal comfort zone. I suggest this guideline. Make yourself
the butt of the joke, but don't be a buffoon. Remember to be
good to yourself.

Handle Audiences
with Humor Power

During a speech, problems with an audience may take three
forms. The trouble is all ours!

1. Our humor bombs. We lose power and attention.
2. Some mechanical or physical interruption occurs. The
    lights go out, the projector won't work, a waiter drops
    a loaded tray.
3. An individual in the audience interrupts, accidentally
    or purposefully.

It's my experience that if we learn to handle humor power,
these problems won't trouble us.

What to Do When Humor Bombs

Humor bombs when it isn't used as a power, when it's tossed
in, not woven in. It fails when we don't know our audience.

We learn by doing. After we try a bit of humor once or
twice, and it still doesn't work, the best thing we can do about
it is to leave it out of our next speech.

In an awkward moment, when humor has failed, laugh at
yourself and with the audience by saying, "It would take the
FBI [or the local police force] to find that joke."

"Let's make a deal. If you'll laugh at that story, I'll agree
not to tell it again." Or: "Before I go any further, I'll make
you an offer. If you laugh at one joke, you get five free."

My TEAM associates and I call lines like these "savers."
Savers can help you, not only on the platform, but in any awk-

ward or embarrassing situation. For example, George Burns has used savers to kid about his age. Asked why he dated so many much-younger girls, he answered, "At my age, what else is there?"

When you need a saver during a speech, try these.

"I know you're out there 'cause I can hear you breathing."

"Am I going too fast for you?"

Or, if you see someone whispering to someone else, "Why don't you explain it to him/her on the way home?"

"Those aren't the greatest examples of humor in the world," comments Art Fettig, who uses savers, too. "They don't need to be. They work for you when an earlier joke falls flat. Laughter is an audience contribution to your speech. You can help your audience contribute!"

Art suggests another saver: "On these occasions, sometimes you get a good speaker, and sometimes you get a rotten one. Today, you get a double treat, because my wife tells me I'm good and rotten."

What to Do About Mechanical Interruptions

When something unexpected comes up in a speech, I turn to a saver to get me off the hook. "It's been a rough day. I had an M&M melt in my hand."

If the projection machine goes out, I might say, "I see the Fairmont Hotel here didn't pay the electric bill."

If something goes wrong and there's a delay, my saver might be, "As they say in the nudist camps, please *bare* with us." I go on to explain South Bend is the home of one of the largest nudist camps, and people come there from all over the world.

"They even have Ivy League nudists. Those are the ones with three belly buttons."

If the delay is long and the audience starts squirming and buzzing, take advantage of the noise. Say, "We've waited so long, I think I hear the buzzards starting to circle over us."

Any small problem or unexpected happening can be smoothed with a saver. "This situation is as hard to handle as an armful of coat hangers."

What to Do About
Individual Interruptions

After lecturing to a tough audience, a speaker was asked, "Did you kill them?"

"No," replied the speaker. "They were dead when I got there."

Yes, audiences can be tough! Every audience is different. Every situation is different. A situation beyond our control may create a tough, even hostile attitude. To change that attitude, it helps to be nice, polite, pleasant—no matter what happens. Remember, humor power will work for us to relax audience tensions.

I believe I'm pledged to make every audience a *good* audience. If there is an interruption, I try to take advantage of it with savers. I ask the individual who interrupted, "What is your name, sir?" If it's an unusual name, I ask, "Is that your real name, or did you make it up?"

Then I kid the individual and try to make him feel at ease. The idea behind that is, most people would rather be kidded than ignored, and virtually everyone would rather be included than excluded. The worst of all insults is to be ignored.

Occasionally, speaker Ken McFarland has a question period following one of his lectures. Once in a while, the floor will be taken over by someone who says he wants to ask a question, but who really wants to make a speech. Such an individual may rattle on for five minutes or more.

When the "questioner" has finally concluded his discourse, Ken will say, "Will you repeat the question, please?" This saver gets a laugh from the audience, puts things back into perspective, and gets the session back on the track.

By accident, we may "interrupt" ourselves! Speaker Dave Yoho gives us an example of how this happens and how to handle such a situation with humor power. Envision him addressing the Sales and Marketing Executives of Raleigh, North Carolina.

About twenty minutes into his presentation, Dave was delivering his message about communication in the sales role.

"Seldom does the prospect give us a yes or no answer," he said. "We construct our language so he can't say yes or no. Because of our fear of rejection, we use words that get a response, like 'I'll think about it,' or 'I'll let you know.' "

Dave kept working to one particular man in the audience, because the man was giving him good responses and strong affirmations. He took the microphone to the man and asked him, "Your customers, your prospects, sir, how often do they give you a yes or no answer?"

A roar burst out in the audience. Dave disregarded it, thinking it might be a response to something he had done with a body action. He repeated the question. "How frequently do your customers or prospects react to a sales presentation with a yes or no answer?"

The roar grew even louder. "By then, I knew something was wrong," Dave says, "so I asked him, 'Sir, what do you do?' "

The responsive individual was a leading member of the SME chapter, a man who was running for public office—and a man who owned six undertaking establishments in that community.

Dave tells us, "My response was, 'When I die, you're not going to bury me. I'm going to be cremated and have my ashes put in an egg timer, so I can keep on working in Raleigh, North Carolina.' "

Let humor power strengthen your message and buoy your entire speech. Then, consider . . .

What to Do When
It's Closing Time

Some speakers, it's said, need closings more than they do introductions! All speakers, you and I among them, need effective closings. The opening and the close are the two most vital parts of any speech. After twenty-five years, I still haven't developed an opening or a close that I'm fully satisfied with. I keep trying lots of approaches. That's what I recommend to you. *Keep trying*.

Two other basic rules haven't changed.

Don't tell your audience you're going to close. Avoid such expressions as "And now, in conclusion." Try not to indicate, by body movements, that you're nearing the end of your speech. The audience will start timing you, instead of listening to you.

Leave the audience wanting more. They will, when your speech is to the point, reasonably brief, buoyed by humor power, and closed effectively.

Should you "leave 'em laughing"? Not always. Some speeches call for a highly serious, highly dramatic close. Others need to be wrapped up with brief humor. What you do depends on the nature of your message, on the type of meeting, and even on the time of day.

Close with humor power when it's relevant to your subject, when the occasion is a banquet or other convivial gathering, and when you're speaking at the end of the day. Refresh your listeners and relieve their fatigue.

"I'm the only [last] speaker, so now we can get on with the entertainment."

"I've eaten so much chicken tonight that instead of sleeping, I think I'll roost."

Most of the time, your close will be more effective when you forget about trying for laughs and try, instead, to awaken a smile of recognition. Express a truth, an aphorism to remember, or a wish for your audience—with gentle humor power.

"Man's best friend is DOG—spelled backwards."

"Time flies. Remember, you're the navigator!"

"If what you did yesterday still looks big to you, you have not done much today."

"It's more important to act your way into a better way of feeling than to feel your way into a better way of acting."

"Not to teach your children to work is like teaching them to steal."

"Acceptance, affection, approval. The three A's keep young adults from becoming delinquents."

"To succeed in this modern age, we need the three G's. Gumption, guts, and go."

Leave your listeners smiling with appreciation. The humor power you apply in the main content of your speech will be contagious, spreading through your close and enduring afterward.

We've discussed several ways of developing your humor power, and in Chapter 7 I suggested some specific ways to "tell a joke." Let me add some do's and don'ts that apply especially to speaking.

DO Set Up Your Story—but
DON'T Telegraph Your Punches

Deliver your humor power with enthusiasm in your voice, authenticity in detail, dramatic buildup, and a little suspense before you give the punch line. An unfunny thing happens en route to some punch lines. A speaker trips over his tongue in his hurry to get to the point. Eager to make others laugh, he telegraphs his punch by letting us know, too early, that something funny is about to happen.

The point of a joke has full effect only when it comes as a surprise to the listener. Remember, not only cats can lick themselves with their tongues!

If a speaker fails to put a joke across, the odds are that he failed to set it up. Set up your vignettes, your anecdotes, even your quips and one-liners. For example, this one-liner works most effectively when there's a pause between its two parts:

"You should go to work for Maytag—as an agitator!"

Mislead your listeners. Don't telegraph the surprise, but

set them up to expect a logical conclusion. With this story don't say, "I'm going to tell you a joke about unemployment." Tell the story!

"Love could end unemployment."

"How?"

"Put all the men on one island and all the women on another."

"So how would that help create—oh, I see. Everyone would start building boats."

Tell your joke slowly enough so that audience expectations can build through misunderstanding—but fast enough so that listeners don't forget your misleading information, or see the surprise too soon.

"He says he's watching his drinking." (Pause) "He only goes to bars that have mirrors."

A wife went to the missing persons bureau to report her missing husband. "He's short and thin, bald, has false teeth." (Pause) "In fact, most of him was missing before he was."

When you tell a joke via the spoken word, your pauses, simple gestures, and voice inflections are the commas, question marks, and exclamation points of written humor. Do punctuate your joke by stressing important words, and pausing after important facts to let them sink in.

A Midwesterner had to make a quick trip to Chicago. He headed out of town in a hurry. Before he hit the highway, he needed information. (Pause)

But only one attended toll booth was open. A long line of cars crawled forward. (Pause)

By the time our friend reached the attendant at the toll booth, he was furious. (Turn your head to "speak to the attendant.")

"How far is it to Chicago?" (Say it with frustration!)

(Turn your head to speak "as the attendant.") "The way you're headed, it's about three thousand, four hundred and thirteen miles."

There's no such thing as a sure-fire joke or a guaranteed laugh. But you'll get more response to your humor power if you set up your story and don't telegraph your punches. After you've told the story, pause again. Don't rush on to the next point or the next story. Give your listeners an opportunity to appreciate your humor power. *Pause to let them laugh.*

DO Watch Your Timing, but DON'T Honk for Humor

When you're telling a joke, how slow is too slow and how fast is too fast? Professional comedians spend hours trying to get the answer to that one. They work hard to polish their timing and make it right.

Essentially, timing is what we've just been talking about— the effective use of pace, pauses, and word inflections to give meaning and emphasis. It isn't necessary to try to rival, or equal, professional comedians, but you can learn about timing by watching and listening to them on TV, radio, or personal appearances.

Good or Great?

Bob Hope considers timing one of his best assets. "At times I have good material, and at other times, I have great material," he explained, "but I know how to cover up the merely good and make it sound great by timing.

"I snap a line, then cover it, then speed on to the next. You have to get over to the audience that there's a game of wits going on, and if they don't stay awake, they'll miss something—like missing a baseball someone has lobbed to them."

Do make your timing as good as you can. Challenge your audience to "see if you can hit this one" with misdirection. For example, say to someone in the audience, "Can you name three animals that Moses took on the ark?" Most individuals tend to miss the point that it was Noah who built the ark! That is, they miss the point—if you don't honk for humor.

Originally, drivers honked their horns to let people know a car was coming. Today, there's always a car coming, so a horn tells people the light is about to change. Speakers who wish to tell stories with humor power do better to observe a "no honking" ordinance. Don't tell your audience what's coming.

The loudest and least desirable honk for humor is to laugh at our own jokes, before, during, or after we tell them. All of us have heard speakers, and even professional comedians, who honked so hard at their own "humor" that the joke was swallowed by their guffaws. Under ideal conditions, the hearer of a joke laughs; the teller does not.

Unbridled gestures, "funny" accents, and efforts to "act funny" also honk for humor ahead. About ninety-nine per cent of the time it doesn't arrive. A good poker face and a developed skill for misdirection will make better vehicles for your humor power.

To watch your timing, watch your audience. Especially after you've made a few speeches, you can begin to see whether you're telling a joke too slow or too fast by the expressions on your listeners' faces. Practice helps, too!

DO Listen to Yourself—
Then Laugh!

Practice telling jokes, and weaving them into your speech, with the help of a tape recorder/player. It beats talking to the bathroom mirror.

After you play back what you've said, you may literally laugh at yourself. In this electronic age, you've probably heard your taped voice—but did you really listen to it? Pay attention to yourself as you sound on tape, because that's how you sound to others. Listen, and try again, until you improve your timing and your entire speech.

Brief humor can be the most difficult to put over with

power. Quip a few quips to your tape recorder, then polish
your performance.

"Do you realize you get more protection when you acquire
a car than you do when you acquire a wife? Think about it.
When have you ever heard of a wife being recalled for defective parts?"

"A friend told me he went to a bar that had only one rest
room. The sign on the door said, 'Please knock. This is an
equal opportunity rest room.' "

"He's pretty fat. If you get on an elevator with him, you
better be going down."

"Serving communion in his church recently, a friend
offered the bread and wine to his young grandson. The boy
looked up and asked, 'Do you have any cookies and chocolate
milk?' "

"My wife was on a ladder doing some painting while I
watched a football game. She said to me, 'Honey, if I fall off
this ladder, will you call an ambulance at half time?' "

Test your timing, too, by telling your tape recorder a more
complex story. Check the way you handle those pauses and
emphasize important words in, for instance, this story:

My wife's third cousin twice removed was obsessed with
the idea he had big feet. No matter what anyone said, Ed *knew*
his feet were big—way too big. The poor fellow couldn't enjoy
life. Ed refused to go anywhere. Afraid his big feet would get
in the way!

At last, Ed was persuaded to see a psychiatrist. He spent
two years—and twenty-five thousand dollars—seeing one psychiatrist after another. Finally, the great day came. A psychiatrist convinced Ed that he *didn't* have big feet.

Ed was delighted. To celebrate, he decided to treat himself to dinner at the finest restaurant in town. He entered and
spoke to the maître d'. "A table for one, please."

"Certainly, sir," said the maître d', "but first, you'll have
to take off your skis."

Taping and listening can help tremendously to develop
your humor power. But don't save all your jokes for your tape
recorder.

DO Try Out Your
Humor Power on Others

Today, Don Hutson of Memphis is a very successful speaker and creator of a cassette course on how to sell. A number of years ago, he asked me what he could do to tell jokes more effectively.

"Try them out on other people, Don," I said. "Try them out on your friends, on cab drivers, on airline stewardesses."

Don singled out what he felt was the important point. "I don't see that many airline stewardesses," he complained.

Find your listeners wherever you can! In my case, humor power has always been part of my speeches, but I'm still working to make it work even better. I do try out my humor power in cabs, on planes, and with my family and my TEAM associates.

Your tryouts will act as a filter to remove elements that aren't relevant or recognized as amusing. As you will in your speeches, weave your humor power into what you're saying.

DO Be a Pro—but DON'T Worry About
Being a Professional Comedian

When you make a speech, use your humor power to do the best, most professional job you can. But don't strive for, or wish for, the skills of a professional comedian. Your job is to be yourself, to sound natural, and to express your humor power as part of yourself.

Politicians, for instance, often use humor. Sometimes it's custom-created for them, and sometimes it's self-created. But politicos who get too good at snapping lines find this hurts their validity. Skeptical audiences refuse to believe in their humor—or in them. Listen, and you'll hear, in political speeches, a switch from professional-sounding humor to the humor power of laughing at one's self.

DO Create Your Tag—and
DON'T Forget Your Titles

As the number of speeches you make increases, people are going to call you something. Be sure they call you something you like! Create your tag. Your tag should say something about you and your message. I can illustrate that with some tags other speakers have been given, or have created for themselves.

Ken McFarland has the tag of "Mr. America Speaker." Cavett Robert, "The People Business." Joe Powell, "Collapse of Time Man." Charlie Jarvis is known as "That Funny Dentist." Art Fettig is "Mr. Lucky." And I'm an "Edu-Tainer."

Reinforce your tag by your titles. The more you speak, the more you're going to need catchy, effective titles for what you say. Like your tag, your titles help to attract audiences.

I still think the best title I ever used was "Are Men More Creative than Women, and Why Not?" Its appeal, I'm sure, came from its reality and validity. In one of my earliest speeches, I asked—and answered—the question "Man, does your wife ever stick to a tedious recipe? Of course not. She creates her own culinary masterpiece. That's just one example. Women have a natural edge on all creative abilities, and men must work to keep up."

Others of my titles have included "Greatness Begins with Being Different," "How to Unravel Your Communications Knot," and "How to Recognize Yourself in a Herd of Elephants." As in constructing humor, three of a kind may win in developing titles. For example, I've used the title, "The I's Have It—Imagination, Ideas, Insights."

Suppose you have your tag, your titles, your humor-powered speeches. Suddenly, you're appearing on the platform often. What happens next? You may decide to become a professional speaker. Welcome! My career as a lecturer began in somewhat the same way. While I was a professor at Notre Dame, I started taking my lectures "on the road."

Today, there are increasing opportunities for speakers, and more people are taking advantage of them. More young people, more women, more people in general have begun to make speaking to audiences a way of life.

Whether you speak professionally, speak occasionally, or never speak in public at all (unlikely!), work to create, develop, and use your humor power. Look for resources to help it grow. You'll find rewards that enrich your life.

9 Develop Rewarding Resources

"Where can I find ideas and resources for my humor power? Is there a list of basic humorous situations and jokes?"

Constantly, I'm asked such questions. The answer, like a lot of things about humor power, is a paradox. Yes, you can find a humor list. But don't expect to gain humor power by looking for it on a list.

Since people laugh at different things, there are several lists. Comedians use lists of subjects and situations that get laughs for them. Joke books group humor material in categories such as "Kids," "Love," "Marriage," "Worry"—ordered alphabetically.

I sometimes use a list. Like this:

Age: Youth is that period when we're all looking for greener fields. Middle age is when we can hardly mow the one we've got.

Education: Assigned to write a story with the word "adult" in it, Freddie wrote, "Adults don't have any fun. Adults just sit around and talk. Adults don't do anything. Nothing is duller than adultery."

Experience: Years of experience: Years spent doing the same thing over and over again, in the same way—probably, the wrong way.

Fat: He got so fat they had to give him his own zip code.

Happiness: Is like an arithmetic class. Every time you get one problem solved, the teacher is waiting to give you another one.

Psychology: A psychiatrist examining a friend probed, "Do you ever hear voices without being able to tell who is speaking or where the voices are coming from?"

"Sure."

"When does that happen?"

"When I answer the telephone."

Religion: He who ignores the collection plate shouldn't complain when the church gets hot.

Women: Many male chauvinists can't understand why the hand that once rocked the cradle is now rocking the boat.

My list, of course, would include several stories, quips, and vignettes in each category. Compile your own list! It can help you classify material mentally, then find humor ideas when you need them in a specific situation.

What's more, your list will help you discover resources for humor, make them your own, and convert them to humor power. I suggest five ways to develop your resources:

1. Tune In on Others

2. Use Your Personal Experiences

3. Look, Listen, and Read

4. See the Signs

5. Borrow—but Be Creative

1.   Tune In on Others

Keep your ears tuned to bits of conversation. Listen to the amusing things people say. Ask your friends for help. You'll find many examples of humor power at work.

I regularly tune in on my family, my TEAM associates, my close friends. They add to my humor-power resources—often by ribbing me. Other speakers, clients, and audiences prove

DEVELOP REWARDING RESOURCES

rewarding when I tune in. Important people in your business or profession can reward you in the same way.

Listen to the amusing things others say. Golf partner Frank Bauer and I get together to play golf in South Bend about twice a month. He always seems to come up with good, new quips—that I can use!

About one of the club members, Frank said, "He's such a perfectionist, if he married Raquel Welch, he'd expect her to cook, too."

About another club member, he quipped, "He's got a lot of young blood, but it's in an old container."

About still another member, he said, "He's been so busy he had to pay a guy to do his jogging."

One of Frank's lines is, "He's so rich, he has water skis that sleep six. And a mobile home with an elevator."

On couples' golf night, I heard him ask a woman, "Is this your husband? How long has he been that way?" As that example shows, Frank Bauer realizes people enjoy being kidded.

Dr. Robert Meyer, my South Bend dentist, helps me with dental-humor stories, like this one.

"We're going to have a fire drill today," Dr. Meyer told a new dental assistant.

The assistant looked puzzled. "What tray will I find the drill in?"

Swapping stories with the people you know and meet gives you a bonus. It seems to add sparkle and believability when you can say, "My friend, Josh or Joy Smiley, told me this story. He/she tells it better than I do, but I'm going to try."

It isn't always necessary to know the person who quips funny. You've probably had the experience of walking along the street and overhearing a bit of conversation, such as, "It wasn't much of a proposal. He asked me if we could unite our pay envelopes."

Be an eavesdropper! This bit of conversation was overheard at the supermarket: "I don't need a cart. All I brought with me is twenty dollars."

Find power in on-the-job humor. Listen to others talk, humorously, about their work. Listen, of course, to your associates. But don't overlook the humor power awaiting you in other fields. Every business or profession has its "inside" jokes —with fresh appeal to those on the outside.

When you meet someone from another field, listen to the funny things he or she says. Swap stories—and swipe stories! As story swipers, we can adapt humor power to our life-styles.

Here are a couple of jokes I swiped from Charlie Jarvis, "That Funny Dentist."

PATIENT: What do I do about yellow teeth?

DENTIST: Wear a brown tie.

PATIENT: I'd like to have my teeth checked.

DENTIST: That's strange. Most people want them white.

Some inside stories offer the opportunity to develop "dumb" jokes. We're lucky when we tune in on a "dumb" story.

JUDGE: What's the charge against this man?

POLICEMAN: Bigotry, Your Honor. He has three wives.

JUDGE: You dumbbell, that's not bigotry. That's trigonometry.

Stories about others' goofs go over well because most people like to feel superior. They also like to feel comfortable—even when they won't admit they goof, too.

For me, listening to other speakers is a "busman's holiday" that I thoroughly enjoy as I improve my humor power. For you, listening to speakers may not be part of your job, but it can certainly help to enrich *your* humor-power resources.

You may pick up unintentional humor from an introduction. "Our speaker's hobbies are hunting, fishing, tinkering with his car and his wife, Nancy."

Listen to speakers for live illustrations of ways to work humor power into your personal, social, family, and job lives. I always gain from hearing Lyle Crist, an English professor and speaker.

Lyle Crist says, "With words, man can think. Without words, he can only emote." He reinforces that message with examples related to careless use of language. Here are three.

"Lettuce will not turn brown if you put your head in a plastic bag."

He talks about a sign: "Quality Dry Cleaners, twenty-eight years on the same spot."

"You'd think," muses Lyle, "the fabric would be worn out by now."

Another blooper Lyle quotes deals with a TV newscast during a space mission. A reporter said, "I see we have a film report of the astronauts' breakfast, which will be coming up shortly."

Many speakers spark their presentations with pithy proverbs or epigrams. Dr. Heartsill Wilson of Denver is known for his thought-provoking humor power. His quotable lines inspire others to develop comparable themes.

"Most people can't tell you their blood type, but ninety-five per cent can tell you their astrological sign."

"Life is like owning a boat. Always something wrong with it."

"There are many formulas for success, but none of them work unless you do."

Humor-powered stories abound in speakers' presentations. I heard George Brown, as lieutenant governor of Colorado, tell the following story, effectively.

Three people were arguing about which profession came first.

"The medical profession, obviously," said a doctor. "God is called the great healer."

The second, an engineer, said, "No, engineers were first, because the Bible says God created the world out of chaos and confusion."

"You're both wrong," the third, a politician, said. "Politicians came first. Who do you think created the chaos and confusion?"

Alert: Build your own humor-powered threesomes. The format of George Brown's story can be reworked to produce:

Three surgeons were bragging about their abilities.

First: I grafted an arm on a man, and now he is one of the best pitchers in the National League.

Second: That's nothing. I grafted a leg on a man, and now he is one of the world's best long-distance runners.

Third: That's nothing. I grafted a smile on a jackass, and now he's a congressman.

Discover your own stories. Tune in to others' reactions. We can be sure we're building our humor-power resources when others reward us by reacting with a humor-powered response. A reward I liked was a note from Joe Bush of Louisville.

Joe had been a member of one of my audiences, and he wrote to tell me, "I would like to share an observation I have made after being married for thirteen years and the father of four children. This occurred to me the other day while shaving.

"Shaving cream is the best *laxative* in the world. Ask any man with a family what happens when he gets all lathered up. Someone has to use the bathroom. It doesn't make any difference if it's 6 A.M., 6 P.M., or 10 P.M.

"Five years ago I caused a massive outbreak of constipation in my family. I grew a beard!"

Joe's genial conclusion appealed to me. He wrote, "Thanks for your time and humor."

A fictionalized letter, phone call, or incident can become the springboard for humor power. One example is a probably fictitious letter to the President—or, perhaps, the mayor or governor. The letter begins by congratulating the President on his achievements. The concluding sentence reads, "Please excuse this letter being written in crayon, but where I am, they won't let me use any sharp instruments."

Bill Gove, a platform master and my mentor for more than twenty years, has used a fictitious letter about a man who wrote to a swinger, "I understand you have been fooling around with my wife. Cut it out." The swinger wrote back, "I got your form letter. I don't know what the other guys want to do, but whatever you work out is okay with me."

As another example, I have said I tuned in this letter: "Dear Dr. True, Your humorous talks are terrific. They'll be remembered long after Mark Twain, Will Rogers, Robert Benchley, and Groucho Marx are forgotten, but not before."

When we tell a story about a fictitious phone call, we can suddenly disappoint our listeners' logical expectations—and reward with humor power.

HUSBAND (answering phone): I don't know. Call the weather bureau.

WIFE: Who was that?

HUSBAND: Some jerk asking if the coast was clear.

Another one goes like this:

HUSBAND (answering phone): She's out. Who shall I say was going to listen?

Find fun in the commonplace. Tune in on life around you. Your humor power gains when you can concentrate it on actual incidents from everyday life. People like to laugh at situations they recognize. If they hear something familiar, they're instantly in a mood to be amused.

My everyday life involves a lot of flying. One line the TEAM uses about me is, "If Dr. True hasn't spoken in your hometown, he has probably flown over it." During all that flying, and some waiting on the ground, I've noticed that airline pilots apply humor power to dreary situations.

On a Delta Airlines flight from Chicago to Raleigh, there was a long ground delay.

"We're delaying here a few minutes because of a survey we've made that finds ninety-six and a half per cent of people like to arrive at their destination with their baggage," Captain Bill Hill announced. "The other three and a half per cent of you don't carry baggage, or you resolve your problems other ways.

"A few people came on different planes today, and we're waiting to make them happy. I just want you to know we're still going to give you same-day service."

When departure time had come and gone, Captain Hill said, "I'll be walking through the back to see that nobody got out during our delay here." Flight attendants Christie Poling, Bonnie Anthony, and Glenn Leppert played their humor-powered part, too, in making the delay bearable, even pleasant.

At the University of Oklahoma, I tuned in to Stewart Harrel, professor of public relations. Speaking to a convention of pharmacists, he wowed and won them with a true-to-life story. They recognized the actual in this situation:

A druggist fell so deeply into debt that his banker summoned him. After a long talk, the druggist inquired, "Have you ever been in the drugstore business?"

"No," said the banker.

"Well," said the druggist, "you are now."

Pharmacists, bankers, and airline pilots may not be part of your everyday life. Funny situations are.

Look around you, and notice the cab that displays this sign: "Please tip generously. Your driver has been declared legally blind."

Find generous portions of think-funny ideas in business operations—restaurants, for instance. Guy Leonard of Golden Gate Restaurant Association, San Francisco, told me of one restaurant operator who says, "Our food is untouched by human hands. We have a baboon for a cook."

Tune in to the auto salesman who tells you, "Yes, we'll give you a trade on your car. We'll give you a ball-point pen for it." Appreciate his tongue-in-cheek humor, along with that of Van Gates, South Bend's Chevrolet dealer, who sells, not used cars, but "the best pre-owned cars."

Tuning in rewards you with the familiarity of situations others were in, then worked out of—with humor power. If you find yourself grinning, chuckling, feeling good inside as others

apply their humor power, make their examples part of your resources.

2. Use Your Personal Experiences

All five ways to develop your humor-power resources are
interwoven, one with the others. Take the rewards of tuning in.
Add your personal experiences. Virtually all involve humor-
powered interaction with another individual.

Since seven of our eight children have been to an orthodontist, my personal experience includes a conversation with
orthodontist Dr. Jack Wright. His humor power made my experience—the conversation—rewarding.

Tongue in cheek, I said to him, "You don't appreciate the
sacrifices we made to pay you two thousand dollars a kid for
thirty-nine cents' worth of wire to straighten teeth."

"That's not true, Herb," Dr. Wright said. "I named my
Learjet after you."

Speaker Roy Hatten of Jackson, Mississippi, relates an experience that helped him increase his humor-power resources.

"I like to collect things that keep me humble," Roy says.
"On one occasion, I checked into the Arizona Biltmore in
Phoenix for a convention. I ran into Paul Harvey, the news
commentator and speaker, who was just checking out. We
chatted, then I headed for my room.

"The bellboy, who had noticed us talking, said, 'You
mean Paul Harvey knows who *you* are?'

"I laughed and answered, 'It strikes me funny, too.'

"The bellboy asked, 'Well, who are you?'

"I didn't have an answer! That question will keep anyone
humble."

Tell about the amusing things that happen, day by day.
They don't have to be big events.

Humorist George Gobel has personalized the commonplace with such remarks as, "My wife and I were sitting
around talking, the way you do when the TV set is busted."

Apply humor power to painful experiences. The ability to
see the funny side of unpleasant situations reveals and enriches
your humor power. What's more, it eases the pain.

One of the best examples I've found came to me from a client, Ken Austin of the Retail Farm Equipment Association in Owatonna, Minnesota. On an early November morning, Ken took a shower—and the next time I saw him, he was on crutches. He gave me a copy of the note he sent out at Christmas to tell people what happened.

"In the shower," Ken's note said, "I dropped the soap, bent to pick it up, slipped, and opened up a gash in my left leg, just below the kneecap and deep enough to sever the patella tendon."

After the tendon and muscles were sewn back together, his leg was put in a hip-to-ankle cast. Later, Ken wrote, "The doctor took the cast off and promptly put on another, just as straight and heavy, and about two inches longer than the first one.

"I have been getting quite a bit of advice on 'what time of the year to take a bath' and 'never take a shower alone.' The thing that has really hurt is the number of people who said they didn't believe I ever took a bath.

"Take my word, 'Be careful in the shower, and have a good and safe holiday season.'"

Hold up a humor-powered mirror to your life. If you have problems, admit it, and reflect the funny side. You'll be rewarded, as you reward others with the warmth of knowing they're not alone in commonplace, embarrassing, or troubled situations.

3. Look, Listen, and Read

Look at and listen to TV and radio comedians, talk shows, night-club acts, plays, musicals, and movies. Save the funny lines! Adopt and adapt them to your personality and life-style.

Movies, for example. I don't remember the name of a movie I saw years ago, but I saved a line from it. "A fellow I know always wanted to meet a girl who already had a fur coat and her appendix out."

Humorous cassettes and records, speakers' cassettes, and even religious cassettes can help fill the humor-power reservoir. Many speakers, including me, offer cassettes—recordings of their presentations or ideas on how to use humor. For example:

Art Fettig's how-to cassette about humor in speaking is my source for two illustrations I think are great. First, he tells a story he tried out on an older friend.

"At a convention, I met a fellow I know. 'I see you brought your wife with you,' I said.

" 'Yes, I did,' he told me. 'I'd rather bring her than kiss her good-bye.' "

Art's friend stared, astonished and unbelieving. "You surely aren't going to tell *that* old story?" he demanded. "Why, I've used that story for twenty years."

Then Art describes an evening spent with the TV set. He picked up fifty good one-liners—but eighteen of them were one-liners he was already using.

Together, those illustrations make a point important to you. As Art puts it, "There isn't that much new or original humor around." Construct your humor power from the many resources available, but make it fresh and original with your perspective. Recycle old stories for new impact, by telling them in your individual way.

Read books, magazines, and newspapers with humor in view. Don't limit your search for resources to joke books and other humor books. Dip into all kinds of books. Biographies, for instance, usually offer amusing anecdotes about the famous —plus favorite stories told by the famous.

In *LBJ: The Way He Was,* Frank Cormier wrote that President Johnson liked to tell this story about Mark Twain.

On a visit to a friend in the country, Twain was walking along a road. He saw a farmer and asked him, "How far is it to Henderson's place?"

"About a mile and a half," the farmer said.

Twain walked farther, until he saw another farmer and repeated the question. The farmer's reply was, "About a mile and a half."

Twain walked and walked. He met still another farmer

and, for the third time, asked, "How far is it to Henderson's place?"

"About a mile and a half," that farmer replied.

"Thank God!" Mark Twain exclaimed. "I am holding my own!"

From books, consumer and trade magazines, and newspapers, cartoons and their gag lines can suggest situations you can twist to fit your humor power. For example:

WIFE (to husband): This Christmas let's give each other sensible gifts like ties and fur coats.

MAN (to psychiatrist): My wife has developed an inferiority complex. What can I do to keep her that way?

MOTHER (after removing the last layer of winter outerwear from a small child): George! He isn't ours!

When it comes to humor resources in popular magazines, *Reader's Digest* leads the way. At the *Digest*, it's a rule. One third of every issue must be powered by humor. Here's an example from the June 1978 issue—a story originally told by Dick Bothwell in the St. Petersburg *Times*.

A man was seen walking across the desert carrying a jug, a loaf of bread, and a car door. Someone stopped and asked him what he was doing with the three items.

"Well, when I get thirsty, I drink some orange juice from the jug," he said, "and when I get hungry, I eat some of the bread."

"What's the car door for?"

The desert walker answered, "In case I get too hot, I roll down the window."

From trade magazines, you can mine a rich vein of inside humor. Many of them have columns devoted to jokes. Joe Miller, my accountant, saves his accounting magazines for me. Accountant Joe Miller says no, he didn't write that famous *Jests*, and if he hears that question one more time . . . An accounting of humor goes like this:

"There are only two kinds of accountants. One makes it

plain that you can't pay for what you want, even though you've earned it. The other explains how you can afford what you don't have the money for, even though you don't deserve it."

In the business world, companies that put up a bulletin board find that humor can humanize even the first kind of accountant. If he sees a picture of Fagin up there on the board, he naturally won't see himself as the Dickens character who specialized in theft. But he may learn something about the importance of laughing at himself.

I try out such stories first on audiences of accountants. If they go over well, I use them in presentations to general audiences.

Along the same lines, ask your convention-going friends to bring you newsletters and reports of meetings they attended. You can tap far-flung resources without ever leaving home.

When you read magazines and newspapers, look for unintentional humor. You'll find mixed-up ideas, typographical errors, and other bloopers. Like these:

News item: During the ice storm on Saturday, Mrs. Jane Marshall slipped on the ice and hurt her somewhat.

News item: A dog bit Miss Gale Smith, just below the Presbyterian church.

Editorial: Recent reports have said a number of university graduates cannot even read or right.

Want ad in university paper: Sweet little old lady wishes to correspond with young male student. Her son. (That one was for real!)

Church news: The pastor will preach, and there will be special sinning by the congregation.

Headline: Attorney General Urges Closer Look at Nudist Colony.

Sports story: This is one of the games we have to win if we go through the season undefeated.

Another sports-page story said, "The coach has resumed direction of the team's spring practice sessions, after having been laid up for several days with a bad coed."

Save bloopers and work them into your humor-powered

vignettes. In your reading, you'll find compilations of funny boners. Add others from your personal experience.

Your office associates might enjoy this one. "We've been authorized to make a monthly advance to Miss Elizabeth Johnson."

Students are a great source of boners. "Salt Lake City is a city where the Morons settled."

Read the ads for other boners. "If you buy a suit from us, you'll soon want one of our topcoats to wear over it."

Here's one from an insurance contract. "This sum will be paid you in a single amount at the time of your death, which we understand is the way you prefer."

Amusing ideas and situations will come to you as you look, listen, and read. Most valuable to your humor power will be those things you personally observe. Look around you, and notice what others are doing with their humor power. You'll find examples in unexpected places.

I looked around and discovered that Spe-Dee Print, a quick printer in South Bend, was demonstrating its services with humor-powered cards. Their cards give simple messages. "Don't be afraid to ask dumb questions. They're more easily handled than dumb mistakes." Or: "Nothing is opened by mistake more often—than the mouth." All of the cards, of course, exemplify the printer's expertise.

At one of the world's busiest airports, Chicago's O'Hare Field, I found humor power in the basement chapel. Regular masses are held there, and appeals for money are slipped into the various weekly prayer books. Here's an excerpt from one appeal.

"Hi. It's Catholic time. Just to prove that this is the Catholic mass in this Interdenominational Chapel, the very Catholic Sunday collection is about to be taken up. Now, isn't that comforting? Doesn't that make you feel at home? Who said everything is changing in the Church?

"We would never dream of putting a limit to your imaginative generosity. Let your spirit soar. There are absolutely breathtaking combinations of singles, fives, tens, even twenties which do just beautifully. Nor would we scorn a check. We're really very big about this. We're also ecumenical; foreign currency is very welcome.

"No matter what your faith, let yourself go. And thanks, very much!"

Another appeal showed a cartoon of a priest carrying a bag marked "Quarters" and a placard, "Welcome to the Underground Church." It read, in part, "The age of specialization has been felt by the Church. You have heard of the Hoodlum Priest, the Junkie Priest, the Hippie Priest, the Night Pastor. There's even the Flying Nun.

"When our red-faced rector, clutching his little bag of quarters, approaches the bank on Monday mornings to deposit the Sunday collection, there is much poking and giggling among the tellers. They just love to greet the Two-Bit Priest.

"Call him what you want, but we must squeeze a minimum of one dollar from each adult here in our unpretentious catacomb. (You'll have to admit it's pretty good service for a buck!)

"O.K. Your big chance is coming. The very Catholic collection is about to be taken. Get in there and win this one for the Two-Bit Priest!"

Your daily life can reward you with personal examples of do-it-yourself humor power. And the more you use your humor power, the more resources you'll need.

The time may come when you'll want to consider subscribing to professional humor services as resources for current humor, international humor, and pertinent humor from the past. I have found all of the following helpful:

JOKES UN-LTD.   P. O. Box 69855
                Hollywood, California 90069
MACK McGINNIS   *Comedy & Comment, McGinnis's Favored Quotes, Truth with Laughter*
                448 Mitchner
                Indianapolis, Indiana 46219
ROBERT ORBEN   *Orben's Current Comedy, Orben's Comedy Fillers*
                Comedy Center, 700 Orange Street
                Wilmington, Delaware 19801

MARTIN A. RAGAWAY　*Funny, Funny World*
407 Commercial Center Street
Beverly Hills, California 90210

4.　See the Signs

As a humor resource, I suppose signs should be classified with looking and reading. Accidentally or intentionally humorous signs have proved so rewarding to me that I naturally think they deserve a place all their own!

With a wealth of humor power, signs lift the load. They show how individuals and businesses handle their problems. One I saw years ago in an Atlanta delicatessen is still a favorite with me. "We have an agreement with the bank. We don't cash checks, and they don't sell pastrami sandwiches."

A sign in the waiting room of a physicians' group read, "Patients will please not exchange symptoms. It gets the doctors hopelessly confused."

In a Beverly Hills doctor's waiting room, a sign capitalized on interest in meditation: "Don't just sit there. Meditate!"

I saw a sign in a Los Angeles apartment window: "Saxophone for Sale." What was funny about that? Nothing—until I saw the sign in the adjoining window: "Thank God!"

A sign in a boatyard got attention, created talk, and built business: "Let us paint your bottom."

Outside a tile and floor-coverings store: "Our customers walk all over us."

In the office of a Detroit judge: "I agree with what you're saying, but I must admit you're wrong."

In a Dublin flower shop: "Send some flowers to the woman you love—and while you're at it, don't forget your wife."

Seen in a Palm Springs restaurant, and accidentally humorous: "Special prices for dinner, five to seven P.M. Remember, the early bird catches the worm."

Posted on a Yale dormitory door: "If I'm studying when you enter, please wake me up."

In an Albany, New York, state government building: "Be yourself! There's nobody better qualified."

Inside an elevator at the World Trade Center: "Button for eighth floor out of order. Push five and three."

On a snack truck: "Love at First Bite."

Scrawled in a subway train: "Just because you're not paranoid doesn't mean they're not out to get you."

On a marriage counselor's door: "Back in an hour. Don't fight."

With creative humor power, signs can help you develop vignettes that persuade and motivate.

The athletics department at one school was having trouble with thefts of T-shirts. But the case of the vanishing shirts was solved—when each one was stenciled across the front with the words "Third String."

"GROJ Sale," the sign announced. Neighbors and strangers flocked to the sale. Most congratulated the seller on his amusing spelling of "garage."

"Oh, no," he protested in surprise. "What it actually stands for is, 'Get Rid of Junk.'"

At the building-materials store, a sign warned do-it-yourselfers, "Just because you know how it all goes together doesn't mean you can put it together." It reads well as a humor-powered caution, applied to daily living.

Start collecting signs! Funny, amusing, or thought-provoking, they will increase your humor power.

5. Borrow—but Be Creative

If you're bothered about borrowing humor from others, don't be! It's virtually impossible for a humor-power application to be totally original. Humor-powerful individuals gain their skill and talent by borrowing, adapting, and working with a wide range of resources.

According to a tongue-in-cheek rule, when you get humor from others, you should give them credit three times. By then, you will have goofed it up so much and made it so thoroughly yours, your sources would be ashamed of it anyway!

A classic story tells of two comedians who were talking together before their act. One said to the other, "If you won't use my Bob Hope jokes, I won't use your Henny Youngman jokes."

To the Park

Said one New Yorker to another, "Can you tell me how to get to Central Park?"
    "No."
    "Okay, I'll mug you here."

—HENNY YOUNGMAN

Just as a one-liner can have two or more lines, stories and quips usually have many parents. Adopt, then adapt! Borrowing jokes doesn't mean you and I use them exactly the way someone else told or wrote them. That would result in flat, unfunny material, for individual perspective and personal approach are at the center of humor power.

Experiment! Unflex your humor-power talents by trying to give a well-worn expression, a famous proverb, or an old joke a new twist.

"He's so obnoxious, you have to get to know him before you can really dislike him." Just be sure "he" will think it's funny, too!

Take the well-known expression "Money isn't everything." Give it a twist by adding, "But what else is?" Or try, "Money isn't everything, but don't let anybody tell you it isn't."

Sammy Kaye is remembered, not only as a musician, but for his humor power, as best revealed in a twist on an old saying, "The oboe is an ill wind that no one blows good."

The proverbs of Poor Richard have undergone many twists and turns since they left Ben Franklin's pen. Try another twist!

"Late to bed and early to rise makes a man unhealthy, poor, and sleepy." No rhyme? The flat ending can add humor power.

Twisting Poor Richard

Early to rise and early to bed makes a man healthy, wealthy, and dead.

—JAMES THURBER

Twisting proverbs and clichés powers humor to make what you say more vivid and memorable. Perhaps the best known of such twists is this classic. Not "All work and no play makes Jack a dull boy" but "All work and no play makes jack." Twist your own!

Not "It was raining cats and dogs" but "It was raining cats and dogs. Fortunately, they were Seeing Eye dogs."

Not "A loaf of bread, a jug of wine, and thou" but "A loaf of pumpernickel, a jug of rye, and thou hast shot the week's bread budget."

Not "A dog is man's best friend" but "A man's best dog will make friends with that gorgeous blonde's terrier."

Twist familiar ideas. "You owe it to yourself to be successful, but when you become successful, you owe it to the IRS."

Again, recycle old but evergreen humor-power items. Does this one sound familiar?

A pompous, puffed-up bore said to a humorist, "Mr. Blank treated me as though I was a fool." The humorist consoled him, "Don't let that upset you. He probably thought you knew it."

Perhaps you've heard similar stories changed, updated, and credited to some well-known person of today. In fact, the humorist in this vignette was Sydney Smith, an English clergyman and author, 1771–1845. Quips from his work can be given a timely twist, too. "What you don't know would make a great book," he wrote. Timely today!

Daniel Webster, Smith said, was "like a steam engine in trousers." The simile is dated, but the image isn't. Updated to "jet engine in pants," it could describe the most dynamic person you know.

About an English politician, Smith quipped, "No one minds what he says. It's not more than a week ago that I heard him speak disrespectfully of the equator." You could follow that pattern, but twist the message. "Good old Joe says some shocking things. About a week ago, I heard him speak disrespectfully of his mother-in-law."

Twist and exaggerate, for hyperbolic humor power. While you're at it, develop some more of those familiar vehicles we discussed in Chapter 7:

"I got so fat because I went on a seafood diet. Whenever I see food, I eat it."

"The farm community I come from is so small, you could always spot a funeral procession. The lead tractor would have its lights on."

"The fish that got away was so big, the fisherman never saw one like it before or since. Or then."

"The movie was so bad, people were standing in line to get out."

Once in a while, it pays to exaggerate negatives. "Our pianos are just as bad as our competitors', and for less money." Start by looking on the bright side, think funny, and twist advantages into humor-powerful disadvantages. Unbelievable, but effective!

That method worked when a "house for sale" was advertised in glowing terms—with no results. Another ad for the same house listed "six tiny rooms; ratty decorations; leaky basement; muddy street; no bus; no furnace; all for $25,000." Ten prospects showed up—because the ad replaced unconvincing exaggeration with an appeal to the spirit of fun and play and the house sold!

Play around with words. Just one word can spark a message, as in this quip and comment on a marriage: "When she goes out to play bingo, bingo!, he goes out to play."

Adding a word often changes the entire meaning of a sentence or a story, and creates humor power. Try this with news items.

"Inflation will be ended," the President promised—again.

With the same technique, develop vignettes.

SECRETARY: I sure feel like telling the boss where to get off again.

CLERK: What do you mean, again?

SECRETARY: I felt like it yesterday, too.

An English teacher tried word play when she wanted to impress her students with the difference between "all ready" and "already." "It's important," she insisted. "Look at it this way. Are you all ready to be kissed, or have you already been kissed?"

When you think funny about words, you can create humor power to help people laugh at themselves.

"This is a pickup band. We call it that because, every time a guy goes to the men's room, the band tries to pick up his girl."

When the door of the crowded bus opened, a good-looking girl looked in and asked the driver, "Can you squeeze me in there?"

"I'd be glad to," said the driver, "but somebody has to drive the bus."

SUPERMARKET SHOPPER: It sure is tough when you have to pay four dollars a pound for meat.

SUPERMARKET MANAGER: Yes, but it's tougher when you pay only two dollars.

Twisting words and exaggerating situations can lead to wacky, zany ideas, for the humor power of the ridiculous.

HUNTER: I shot an elk today.

WIFE: Are you sure it was an elk?

HUNTER: Of course I am. I saw his membership card.

When a man with a bleeding ear and alcohol breath asked a doctor to treat his ear, the dialogue went like this: "What happened to you?"

"I bit my ear."

"How did you do that?"

"Well, I stood on a chair."

Another dizzy dialogue: "I can't live with my wife any-more. She wants to keep a goat in our bedroom."

"Why don't you just open the window?"

"What! And let all my pigeons fly out?"

Understate, for the humor power of the underwhelming, and you can come up with stories of this type:

TOURIST: Were any big men born around here?

OLD-TIMER: Nope. Best we can do is babies.

When you're twisting words, remember names. You can make stories funnier, from the beginning, by tagging a char-acter with a memorable name. Effie Clinker. Gomer Cool. Elsie Crack. Drizzle Puss, brother of Chief Rain in the Face.

Always tagging the bald-headed man "Curly" or the human beanpole "Shorty" is a humor technique as old as time. Old and corny? Of course! But it's effective.

Don't be afraid to be corny. Listen to Red Skelton, whose wealth of vital energy comes forth in performing his act, paint-ing clown portraits, singing, composing musical pieces, writing and—as spare-time hobbies!—bookbinding and gardening.

Early in his performing career, Red, honestly puzzled, asked, "If I'm so hokey and corny, how come people keep stealing my material?"

His grandmother told him, "What's the matter, you gettin' lazy? You can think them up faster than anyone can steal them."

I am rather proud of the fact that I've seen Red Skelton live more than twenty times—six times in one year! I've watched him on TV, of course, and I saved a line from one of his shows, many years ago. "I don't like to go to doctors and get blood tests and all that stuff—because of my back. I've got a yellow streak right up the middle of it."

Red has summed up his "corny" approach this way: "People watch me, and they see things familiar to their lives. They see people they know."

Be corny—and authentic! Take familiar situations, add a twist, and you're on your way to still another kind of story:

The plumber promised to fix the little leak within twenty-four hours. Three days later, he waded in. When the householder complained, the plumber was indignant. "Twenty-four hours *is* three days," he declared. "I work an eight-hour day."

If you need a humor resource in a hurry, to fit a specific message or make a special point—and you can't find what you want—you can often create one quickly with a switch in the setting of a joke. Here, for instance, a story about salesmen moves to a restaurant and becomes a story about waitresses:

A psychiatrist was asked, "Do intelligent waitresses [salesmen] make good wives [husbands]?"

His opinion: "Intelligent waitresses [salesmen] don't get married."

Others' humor may remind you of stories and quips you heard long ago. For example, another of my golf partners is Warren McGill, a lawyer and a master of the self-directed insult. Warren has the power to laugh at himself with remarks like this one:

"Anybody who takes me for a fool makes no mistake."

His self-focused insult helped me remember and recycle some humor-power resources of the insulting kind. I've always felt that this kind of humor can be used effectively *if* it's used playfully and in fun.

The humor of the insult takes two forms. First, the self-insult often reveals an element of truth about one's self. And the second form involves a conversation or dialogue with one person delivering the pretended insult and the other receiving it. For example, this dialogue:

"I've got a splinter in my finger."

"What's the matter, been scratching your head?"

In a vignette about an insult, a professional craftsman visited a friend who was making some do-it-yourself home repairs. "Your work reminds me of lightning," the pro commented.

"Because I'm so fast?" queried his friend.

"No. Because you never strike twice in the same place."

Under the surface of insulting humor lies the power to convey such messages as: "All of us make mistakes"; "Try laughing at yourself"; and "Don't take yourself too seriously."

Nowadays, when you look forward to adopting some quips from a pro and adapting them, you may hear fewer one-liners. Many of the new funny people—Steve Martin, for instance—prefer the humor of the absurd. This humor may be philosophical, shrewd, even stinging. It's seldom pithily pointed, in the manner of the one-liner.

When I caught Andy Kaufman at The Comedy Store in Los Angeles, I noted just one quip or one-liner in his two-hour presentation. He said he was going to do one of the big Elvis Presley records.

"It was Elvis's biggest record," Andy explained. "Well, actually, all of Elvis's records were the same size."

The humor of the absurd makes a point for all who would be humor-powered. It's the kind of humor we need to collapse high hats and deflate pomposity. What's more, it reminds us that humor is precious, a rare treat, and not to be overused.

Express your humor power—and be proud you're not the pest who heaps funny line on funny line till he smothers them, every one.

Borrow, and be creative. Understand the dynamics of fun. Work regularly with humor material, and you will develop your own funny ideas and situations. Inspiration will strike— usually, when you're working the hardest!

Thinking funny helps considerably, as Jim Pickens of Mishawaka, Indiana, knows. A speaker and artist, Jim has developed a humor-powered philosophy keyed to thinking funny.

"'Think funny' is a two-word tonic to soothe the symptoms of irritation," Jim says. "It's an attitude, a state of mind —and it's of most value in helping us live with ourselves."

Jim thinks funny about himself. He claims he's "the guy with a great speech right in the hollow of his head." He declares that he has been "an artist, writer, salesman, teacher, businessman, and cartoonist—proving only one thing. He can't hold a job." As a speaker, Jim maintains he doesn't know any new jokes. Who does? He recycles jokes.

Here's one of Jim Pickens' recycled stories, powered by think-funny humor:

A fellow walked up to a coffee-vending machine, put in money, pressed coffee, sugar, and cream buttons, and looked down. No cup!

As he watched the whole works flow away, he said, "That's what I call automation. Durn machine not only gives you coffee, sugar, and cream. It drinks it for you."

We've examined five ways to build your humor resources, the raw material of your humor power. What do you do with the raw material?

Clip it, copy it, make a note of it. Clip newspapers and magazines. Make copies of material that can't be clipped. When you hear a good story, make a note of it. Be sure you get the details and the punch line right.

My friends and associates rib me because I often whip out a three-by-five card and jot down anything funny I hear. For instance, some of my best stories come from members of my audiences. I have also formed the habit of keeping a notebook or cards handy when I'm watching a movie, a night-club act, or any performance that may contain funny ideas and lines.

You may have a memory better than mine. That wouldn't be difficult! A line I use to *prove* it is, "I have taken the Sam Carnegie speakers' course four times." I wanted to tell you about the line, because it's also an example of the kind of humor that builds through repetition. The more often I use it, the more laughs it gets.

But I ran into a problem. I couldn't remember "Sam" Carnegie's real first name—had to ask a TEAM associate for help. That's the truth! I had used "Sam" for so long, I forgot that, of course, his name was *Dale* Carnegie.

Humor power does help us to remember. Still, I think anyone can benefit from making notes of humor material.

File it—but don't just file it. File your raw material on cards, or record it. Set up categories any way you wish. They can cover subject matter—age, education, politics, for instance

—or types of jokes—anecdotes, epigrams, puns, stories. You decide!

Don't just file your material away. Reread it, or listen to it, often. Interpret attitudes, ideas, and situations in terms of your experience. Keep your reservoir of humor power brimming, ready for instant use.

Observe, study, practice, experiment, work. You will be rewarded with your personal approach to humor power.

Above all, think funny. When you think funny enough, the humor power bursts out in all directions. Start with a willingness to see the funny side. Take a different view of the commonplace. More than any other resource, your think-funny perspective will boost your humor power!

10 Humor Power —Yours!

Awaken your humor power, bring it forth, and make it shine!

Let the guidelines and examples I have shared with you serve as the beginning. Then, remember: *You* generate the highly personal power of humor. Your ability to create, develop, and use humor power exists, just as certainly as your ability to enjoy a good book, a good meal, and a good laugh.

I don't promise you it will be easy, filled only by sunshine and smiles. It's tough to create humor power. You have to work. I do promise my suggestions will work—if you work at them. But you have to do it yourself. And you can.

The first time you use your own humor power in the right way, you won't find an increase in your next paycheck. But you will gain. Humor power works by a universal law of probability. The more you develop and use it, the more it becomes part of your personality, and the more rewards it will bring you.

Consider just a few of those rewards.

Set Yourself Free

With humor power, set yourself free to feel better about yourself and to cope with painful burdens. In the process, you'll discover the freedom to be yourself, be different, and make a difference.

Auguste Renoir, the French Impressionist painter, suffered from crippling arthritis. Yet he painted—even when his painting hand had to be strapped to a brush.

To those who asked how he could work when his pain was so great, this dedicated artist replied, "The beauty remains long after the pain has passed."

To each of us, humor power opens the freedom to remember the joy in a painful moment, occasion, or situation, long after we have forgotten the pain. Through such freedom, we can make a difference in the world around us.

LaVonne and Danny Scheurich of Lancaster, Pennsylvania, were worried about their children's safety in traffic—specifically, the heavy traffic on Stroudsburg Pike, near their home. So the Scheurichs put up a sign.

Immediately, the sign brought results. Cars slowed, then crawled. Some drivers even stopped.

The sign? It said, "Caution! Nudist Crossing."

Generate Vital Energy

With humor power, relax and revitalize yourself and others. Most people think of fatigue as being physical. More often than not, mental and/or emotional stress on top of physical weariness compounds the problem. A humor-powered approach refreshes.

Recharge your batteries with the story of the American couple who toured Scotland and Ireland and, while traveling, compared the merit of Scotch and Irish whiskeys.

"Irish whiskey is stronger," pronounced husband Roger. "One night, Jennifer and I drank a quart of it. The next morning, we got up and went to six o'clock mass."

"How does that prove Irish whiskey is stronger?" challenged a Scot.

Roger answered, "Both of us are Baptist."

With vital energy, inventor Thomas Edison worked long

hours, slept little, and gave catnaps credit for refreshing him. I believe his humor power helped.

While Edison worked to make the incandescent light bulb a practical reality, unimaginative and humor-powerless persons laughed at him. His problem: develop an efficient filament for the bulb. As a start, he tried about twelve hundred different materials.

"You have failed," said his critics, "twelve hundred times."

"Not at all," Edison retorted. "What I have done is to discover twelve hundred materials that won't work."

Let humor power give you the vital energy to reach your goal!

Make Yourself Memorable

With humor power, great people become great, and are remembered.

"Let us endeavor," suggested Mark Twain, "to live so that when we come to die, even the undertaker will be sorry."

A tall tale from ancient times illustrates the value—and the memorability—of humor power. At age seventy, an Oriental was pleased and proud to father a son. Naturally enough, he named the son Age.

After a year, a second son was born. Again, the aged father glowed with pride. He named this son Study.

Another year passed, and a third son arrived to gladden the heart of the ancient one.

"At my age," he said, "this is getting humorous." So he named that son Humor.

The three sons grew and flourished until, one day, their father decided to test their powers. He sent them out to pick up sticks for firewood.

Later, he asked his wife, "How well did they do?"

Their mother reported, "Age brought us a few sticks. He said he got tired of doing the same thing over and over.

"Study didn't pick up any sticks at all. He said he was thinking and forgot what he was doing.

"But we don't have to worry about firewood. Humor brought in a huge stack of sticks."

Experience and education serve a purpose, but humor picks up the load—and will be remembered.

Achieve Greatness

Through humor power, we discover greatness can grow from little things. Greatness may be the art of achieving the impossible, but humor power helps us distinguish between the impossible and the absurd.

As the news flash said, "Man, attempting to walk around world, drowned."

Greatness may grow from teamwork. Humor power helps us rely on others.

On a sunny day, a small girl and a smaller boy walked slowly along the street. The boy's eyes were tightly closed. Holding his hand, the girl guided him.

"What's wrong?" a watcher asked. "Did your brother hurt his eyes?"

"Oh, no, we're just going to the movies," the girl explained. "He shuts his eyes, and I lead him. When we get inside, he opens his eyes in the dark and finds us a couple of seats."

Great teamwork!

With humor power, we show greatness—by showing humility, and focusing on others.

Winston Churchill was slated to broadcast an important speech. Hailing a cab, he told the driver, "Take me to the BBC studios."

"Sorry, can't do it," the driver said. "I just have time to get home, so I can listen to Churchill's speech."

Delighted, Churchill presented the driver with a pound note.

Equally delighted, the driver exclaimed, "To blazes with Churchill! Hop in."

That story is ours to enjoy only because the great Churchill—with humor power—told the joke on himself.

Inspire Others

With humor power, you can develop your powers of leadership and inspire others to participate.

When Dad said, "Eat your Brussels sprouts," the little boy dared him, "Motivate me!" Dare to motivate others, through humor power.

Arthur Brisbane is remembered for his greatness as a newspaper editor and editorial writer. He once sent a young reporter to interview a famous man and ask him a few searching questions.

"I'm scared," the reporter admitted. "How can I ask these questions of that important man?"

"Don't worry, son," Brisbane counseled. "Just imagine you're talking to him while he's wearing his nightshirt."

More recently, Phillies pitcher Steve Carlton teetered just a game away from entering baseball record books as a winner of two hundred games. He teetered for a month, unable to win a game and clinch his record.

Catcher Tim McCarver relaxed Steve's tension and inspired a winning effort. "Let's forget about your two hundredth win," Tim suggested, "and go for two hundred and one."

Spark Courage

With humor power, ignite the vital spark of courage in yourself and those around you. Help others raise their spirits and soften harsh reality.

This, too, takes daring. Probably, the most daring individual was the one who first looked at a chicken and said, "Whatever comes out of that, I'll crack open and eat."

It's tough, but it's true. Getting to the one-yard line doesn't add a thing to the score. Let humor power help you travel that extra yard and gain your goal!

When the goal is freedom, the peoples of many nations have sparked their courage with humor power.

Our nation's founders pioneered the tradition of facing up to grim dangers with humor power in their hearts and freedom ahead. They set the example we've followed ever since Ben Franklin spoke for the signers of the Declaration of Independence: "We must all hang together or assuredly we shall all hang separately."

Where freedom is threatened or dictatorship rules, humor's power sparks courage. Russians find something to smile about in this riddle:

"What nationality were Adam and Eve?"

"Soviet citizens, of course. Nothing to wear, only an apple to eat—but living in Paradise!"

Move Ahead with Humor Power

Lift barriers, lighten loads, risk a little, rise above limitations —and keep on going, with humor power.

Speaker George Bailey recalls a day, many years ago, when he was banking some checks from his performances. He chatted with the teller, Sue Moyes.

Sue smiled, and George smiled. Then George wondered.

"Sue," he asked, "am I smiling because I'm banking checks, or am I banking checks because I'm smiling?"

Something to think about!

Have Fun

Humor power energizes and rewards you, as you inspire and achieve. But keep this in mind: Use your humor power *because it's fun*. If the Lord meant us to be on our toes all the time, He wouldn't have given us so much to sit down with!

During a medical checkup, an octogenarian said, "Doctor, you remember that list of problems you told me I'd have to learn to live with—my arthritis, my weak eyes, my bad hearing, my high blood pressure?"

"Trust me," said the doctor. "You'll learn to live with all your problems."

"I know," the old man agreed. "Now, I was wondering. Could you add a twenty-year-old wife to that list?"

Put having fun with humor power on your list and learn to live happier. Take yourself lightly, and your job in life seriously. Make humor power yours!

Release and reveal your unique Perspective, Opportunity, Winning, Effective, Results. Throw your POWER switch, punch your humor button, rev up your "laugh at yourself" engine. Renew and reward yourself—with humor power.